Men Can Get Embarrassed, Too!

Confusing English Vocabulary
for Spanish Speakers

RICHARD FIRSTEN

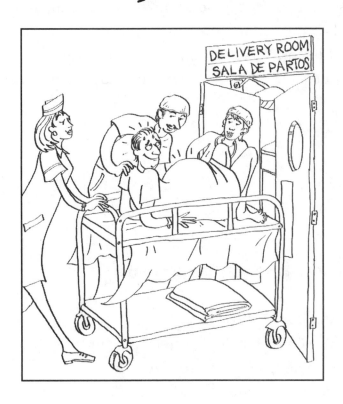

Acquisitions Editor: Aarón Berman
Project Editor: Leland Northam
Manuscript Reviewer and Editor: Prof. Julio Padilla P.
Production Editor: Jamie Ann Cross
Cover Art and Interior Art: Andrew Lange Illustration
Book Design: Solomon Faber & Mary Lambert

The publisher wishes to acknowledge and thank Jackie Flamm
and Prof. Adela Robles Sáez for their suggestions and guidance.

Alta Book Center Publishers - San Francisco
14 Adrian Court
Burlingame, California 94010 USA
Phone: 800 ALTA/ESL • 650.692.1285 – International
Fax: 800 ALTA/FAX • 650.692.4654 – International
Email: info@altaesl.com • Website: www. altaesl.com

ISBN 1-882483-81-2
Library of Congress Card Number: 00-105912

Table of Contents

Section I. Words We Use Often

Section 2. Words We Use Sometimes

Preface

In learning English, one of the most annoying problems comes up when two words look the same or are almost the same in Spanish and in English, but they have very different meanings. If the English student isn't very careful, he or she will invariably use this word incorrectly.

That is why this book exists, so that Spanish speakers do not get so confused. The confusion that they go through only arises because no one has clearly explained to them the differences between these *false*, or *deceptive cognates*, as linguists call these words. This book will be your guide, and if you study the meanings of these tricky words diligently, you will avoid most of the misunderstandings. You will also find in this book many other words that create problems for English students.

Educated native speakers of English tend to use more words derived from Latin and Greek than from Anglo-Saxon when they want their speech to sound very formal. Because of the historical development of English, words from Anglo-Saxon tend to sound more informal or colloquial to English speakers. Therefore, there may actually be fewer deceptive cognates between Spanish and formal English than between Spanish and informal, or colloquial, English. It should be mentioned, however, that when this phenomenon of vocabulary choice occurs, native English speakers tend to use more Anglo-Saxon vocabulary in everyday speech.

Please remember that the focus of this book is on the most common, regularly used meanings of the words listed. There may very easily be secondary and even tertiary meanings which could be the same in English and in Spanish, but that is not the reason for this book. The words which have been chosen here are those that cause the most confusion between the two languages based on their primary meanings alone.

One further point which should be made clear is that not every Latin American country uses each and every Spanish word the same way, a phenomenon which occurs within every language. There may even be variations in meaning from one region of a country to another, let alone from one country to another. So if you come across a Spanish word in this book that is not defined the way it is used in your country, keep in mind that it has that meaning in other countries.

In closing, please remember that if you master these tricky words, you will not become confused if a man says to you, "I'm embarrassed." You will understand that he is *apenado*, not *embarazado*!

Richard Firsten

Richard Firsten
Miami, Florida, USA

Prefacio

Existe un grupo de palabras que, aunque se escriban de manera similar en español y en inglés, tienen significados diferentes en ambos idiomas. En lingüística se las conoce con el nombre de cognados falsos o equívocos. A pesar de su importancia, no se les suele dedicar la atención necesaria en el aprendizaje del inglés. Saber usarlos de manera correcta es la única manera de evitar los malentendidos que provocan. Ése es precisamente el propósito del presente libro: ser una guía para evitar que los hispano-hablantes tropiecen con estos falsos cognados.

En él también aparecen las palabras que más problemas dan a los alumnos angloparlantes. Pero las dificultades no son simétricas. Debido a la evolución de la lengua inglesa, las palabras de origen anglosajón suelen parecer más informales o coloquiales a oídos de los angloparlantes. Los hablantes con mayor nivel educativo tienden a utilizar más términos derivados del latín y del griego que de raíz anglosajona cuando quieren que su habla resulte formal. Por lo tanto, hay menos cognados engañosos entre el español y el inglés formal que entre el español y el inglés coloquial o informal. Siempre es bueno recordar que, ante un doblete, los hablantes nativos de inglés suelen preferir el término de origen anglosajón para el habla normal.

Se debe tener presente que este libro se basa en el significado más aceptado y común de las palabras en él utilizadas, aunque en muchos casos haya acepciones secundarias o terciarias de los términos que coincidan en ambos idiomas, dado que el objetivo de este libro es incidir en aquellas palabras cuyos significados principales provocan problemas de traducción.

Asimismo, es necesario recordar que no todas las variantes latinoamericanas dan el mismo significado a cada vocablo. Al igual que ocurre con todos los idiomas, pueden darse variaciones regionales y, por supuesto, entre los distintos países. Por este motivo, algún lector puede encontrar un término definido de manera diferente a la que es de uso habitual en su país.

En cualquier caso, gracias al dominio de estas palabras engañosas, no nos sorprenderemos mucho la próxima vez que un hombre nos confiese que está *embarrassed*, ya que fácilmente entenderemos que lo que está es apenado, y no embarazado.

Richard Firsten

Richard Firsten
Miami, Florida, USA

A modo de prólogo...

– Mrs. Cepero, Ramiro and Luis have been molesting me, – me quejé yo con la ingenuidad propia de un niño hispanohablante en su primer nivel de inglés. La señora Cepero me miró preocupada y luego se sonrió con la complicidad clandestina de quien también sabe hablar español.

– Ya veo que tu inglés va mejorando, — me dijo. Tardé varios años y muchas clases de inglés en entender esa sonrisa y las diferencias de significado entre "molest" y "molestar" (página 148).

Fue gracias a la señora Cepero, al Everglades Elementary School de Miami, Florida, y a otros de mis profesores como Aarón Berman, editor del presente libro, que aprendí a aprovechar las similitudes morfológicas, sintácticas y semánticas entre el inglés y el español sin caer en las trampas de estos falsos cognados. Gracias a personas como ellos, miles de anglohablantes evitan quedarse "embarazados".

Cuando el hispanohablante decide aprender inglés, se aferra a todas aquellas palabras y estructuras gramaticales que le resultan familiares. La gran sorpresa viene cuando nos damos cuenta de que la misma palabra significa cosas diferentes en ambos idiomas y, entonces, "por hacer bonito, hacemos feo".

La lectura del libro de Richard Firsten pone de manifiesto estas interferencias que la semántica denomina "falsos cognados". Viajando por este libro usted se ahorrará muchas de las "molestias" que oscurecen el significado de sus enunciados. Espero que este libro se convierta en su "First-ten book" entre la complicidad, el oportunismo y la corrección lingüística.

Julio Padilla Pérez
Profesor de Inglés
Escuela de Idiomas
Universidad de Antioquia
Medellín, Antioquia, Colombia

Además...

Ameno y divertido, útil e informativo, generador de buena comunicación son los términos que mejor describen esta nueva publicación de Alta Book Center, que por su naturaleza, nace con el sello del éxito.

Su autor, Richard Firsten, merece un reconocimiento especial por depositar en manos de todas las personas que usamos el idioma inglés en nuestro quehacer cotidiano la compilación más completa de falsos cognados conocida hasta ahora – y que de desconocerlos, invariablemente nos pondrían en más de una situación embarazosa frente a nuestros interlocutores.

Y es que el valor de esta herramienta que nos regala Firsten radica en la utilidad que representa, tanto para el hispanohablante que empieza a dar sus primeros pasos en el aprendizaje del inglés, como para el que ya ha alcanzado un nivel avanzado de fluidez y descubre que aún debe refinar sutilezas semánticas si desea asegurar una comunicación adecuada y exitosa. Estas páginas se convierten entonces en fuente indispensable de formación de vocabulario para TODOS – los que aprenden el idioma y los que lo enseñamos - porque al recorrerlas no podemos evitar identificarnos con muchas de las situaciones que tan hábilmente describe el autor y donde sabemos que nos hemos colocado en más de una ocasión...

Men Can Get Embarrassed, Too! no es un libro de referencia adicional para nuestra biblioteca. Será el fiel compañero de páginas gastadas por un uso permanente que trasciende cursos y programas de inglés. Y además... ¡volver a él siempre nos asegurará una dosis gratificante de humor!

María Eugenia Flores, M.A.
Directora Académica
Centro Cultural Costarricense-Norteamericano

Profesora de Inglés
Escuela de Lenguas Modernas
Universidad de Costa Rica
San José, Costa Rica

Acknowledgements

I would like to thank the following individuals for helping so much in the creation of this book:

First of all, Aarón Berman and Simón Almendares for their belief in me and my writing, and all the support they have given towards the publication of this work.

Next, I would like to thank Leland Northam and Jamie Cross, my marvelous editors, for all of their constructive suggestions and light-hearted spirit. Their enthusiasm for this book was greatly appreciated, as was all of their help.

Finally, I must thank Bruce Carl Fontaine for his undying patience and support. He is the wind beneath my wings.

SECTION 1
Words We Use Often

Unit 1: People and Other Living Things

My Word!

assassin   a person who has killed a human being for religious or political reasons

Lee Harvey Oswald was the only assassin in the death of John F. Kennedy.

 NOTICE!

A person who has killed a human being for other than religious or political reasons is called a *murderer.*

He went to the electric chair because he was a murderer. He'd shot his neighbor.

to assassinate   to kill someone for religious or political reasons

A few years ago, somebody tried to assassinate the Pope.

 NOTICE!

To kill someone for other than religious or political reasons is *to murder.*

He murdered his mother-in-law by poisoning her.

casualty   a person who is injured or killed in time of war or a disastrous accident, such as a plane crash or ship that has sunk

There weren't many casualties in that factory chemical explosion.

 NOTICE!

In English, **casualidad** is *accident* or *chance.* In fact, the expression **por casualidad** is *by accident* or *by chance* in English.

We met by accident/by chance at the mall.

conductor   1. leader of an orchestra

A conductor interprets the music while leading an orchestra.

2. a person in charge of everything on a passenger train except the driving of the train

You can usually buy a train ticket from the conductor while you're on the train.

 NOTICE!

In English, the Spanish word **conductor** is *motorist* or *driver*, a person who drives a car.

Because of road construction, drivers are advised not to use King's Highway at this time.

to conduct   to lead or direct an orchestra

It takes special talent to conduct an orchestra.

director   This word is the same in both languages, but in English it rarely means the person who leads an orchestra; in that case, he/she is a conductor. The director of an orchestra usually takes care of their business matters and trips to visit other cities.

Ms. Peabody is the new Director of Marketing at our company.

to direct   to lead or give instructions

The school principal directed the visitor to move his car from the school bus stop.

editor   a professional who works together with writers
On books, the editor helps the author by correcting mistakes and sometimes making changes that the author agrees to. On newspapers and magazines, the editor is in charge of what is finally published.

Leland Northam and Jamie Cross are the editors of this book. They helped Richard Firsten to prepare the text for publication by offering suggestions and making corrections.

NOTICE!

In English, the Spanish word **editor** is *publisher*, the person or company that produces a book for distribution to bookstores, etc.

Alta is the publisher of this book.

to edit   to change text; to prepare something for publication

She's edited three books for Alta Book Center Publishers.

NOTICE!

In English, the Spanish word **editar** is *to publish*.

Which company publishes this magazine?

editorial   an article in a newspaper that expresses the opinions of the paper or the publishers

Have you read the editorial in today's paper about that scandal in

...h word **editorial** can be *publishing house*.

...mall publishing house now, but it's growing every day.

...he/she is the greatest and most important person in

...hings, Hitler and Mussolini were extreme egotists.

...on who doesn't want to share anything with others is ...otist.

...ive me some of your cake? That's very selfish.

maestro   an honorary title given to a musical expert, especially an orchestra conductor (in English, pronounced like "*my-stro*")

Ah, Maestro, your interpretation of Beethoven's 6th Symphony is superb!

 NOTICE!

In English, the Spanish word **maestro** is *teacher*.

My father is the biology teacher in that high school.

mayor   the most important political leader of a city or town

The mayor of New York City has the second hardest political job in the United States. The first, of course, is the President.

 NOTICE!

1. In English, the Spanish word **mayor** means *greater, larger,* or *older/oldest*.

Jennifer is your oldest daughter, isn't she?

2. The Spanish word **mayor** can also mean *major,* a rank in the military.

The rank of major is one step higher than captain.

parents   mother and father

Her parents are retired now and live in South Florida.

 NOTICE!

In English, **parientes** are *relatives* or *relations*.

I don't have any relatives in this area. My whole family is in Oregon.

relations   1. members of your family (a synonym for *relatives*)

I don't have any relations in this city. My whole family is in Iowa.

2. *To have relations* can have a sexual meaning.

That "Casanova" has had relations with many of the women in this office.

3. how groups or countries act with each other

Relations between the governments of the United States and Russia have always been difficult.

NOTICE!

1. In English, the Spanish word **relación** is *relationship,* which means how two or more people act with one another.

I have a very good relationship with all of my neighbors.

2. *Relationship* also means the connection between two or more people.

"What's Jim's relationship to your brother?"
"They were co-workers for many years."

scientist a person who has expert knowledge of one or more sciences

The discoveries that scientists make help us understand our universe.

NOTICE!

The English word *scientific* is an adjective and *scientist* is a noun (the person).

A scientist only uses scientific methods to see if a hypothesis is true or false.

Going  Blank

Here is a list of the words you have just learned. Use them in the blanks that follow. Don't use a word more than once. Enjoy.

assassin	conductor	editor	mayor	parents	relationship
casualties	director	egotist	murderers	relations	scientists

1. My brother thinks he's the greatest architect in our city. The whole family wishes that he weren't such a/an _____. He should be more modest.

2. I love Christmas. I always travel back to my hometown for the holiday so that I can spend it with my _____ and all of my other _____.

3. During the fighting in Kosovo, there were many civilian _____.

4. The most infamous _____ in U.S. history was John Wilkes Booth, the man who killed Abraham Lincoln.

5. _____ say that we will have a colony on Mars sometime in the next century. Wouldn't that be exciting?

6. Ludwig von Beethoven was a wonderful pianist and composer, but he was also a great _____ and led the Vienna Symphony Orchestra for years.

7. In many countries, _____ receive sentences of life in prison for their crimes instead of capital punishment.

8. "Why do you look a little sad today?"

   "It's because my _____ thinks I should make some big changes to my manuscript."

9. "It's wonderful to see you and Jim together with your children. You're such a happy family."

   "Thank you. My husband and I have always had a very good _____ with the children based on love, honesty, and trust."

10. I'm so glad I voted for Cynthia Kennedy in the last city election. She's been a very good _____ who's done many things to help our citizens.

11. "Congratulations on your promotion!"

    "Thank you very much. I hope I do a good job as the new _____ of the Intensive English Program."

ALTA BOOK
CENTER
PUBLISHERS ID

14 Adrian Court
Burlingame
California, 94010
USA

Luis Quintero

Let's I.D. Them!

This is an identification (I.D.) exercise, so you will be using all the words you have just studied. You can work on your own or with a partner. The exercise is on this page and the next page. If you work with a partner, one of you will work exclusively with this page and the other one will work only with the next page. If you work with a partner, choose your page. Now get started.

Here is what to do if you work with a partner. If not, just write in your answers on both pages.

- Read No. 1 to your partner and write down his/her I.D. on the line provided.

- Then your partner will read No. 2 to you. You make the I.D. and he/she will write it down just as you did.

- Now you read No. 3 and keep working this way until you are finished. Wait for your teacher to review the correct answers and then score your partner's answers.

Each answer = 10 points.

Exercise 1-A   I.D.

1. These people are your mother and father.   _____

3. Mary is 14, Ann is 12, and Simon is 10.
   Mary is my . . . child.   _____

5. This person tells musicians in an orchestra how to play.   _____

7. This is somebody who doesn't like to share with others.   _____

9. This is someone who investigates the natural world.   _____

Exercise 2-A   I.D.

1. This kind of company makes books, magazines, etc.   _____

3. This means to murder someone for political reasons.   _____

5. This person is a city's top politician.   _____

7. This can mean how two countries behave with each other.   _____

9. This expression means *por casualidad* in English.   _____

Score: _____ **points**

Read the instructions on the previous page and you'll know what to do. Remember, when you score your partner's answers or your own, each one = 10 points.

Exercise 1-B   **I.D.**

2. This person controls a company, hospital, department, etc.   _____

4. This person helps a writer.   _____

6. This person thinks he is the greatest in the world.   _____

8. This person has killed somebody for political reasons.   _____

10. This is someone who is hurt or killed in an accident   _____
    or a war.

Exercise 2-B   **I.D.**

2. This is somebody who works on a train.   _____

4. In general, this is a person who kills somebody deliberately.   _____

6. This is an article expressing a newspaper's opinions.   _____

8. This means to manufacture a book and put it on the market.   _____

10. This can be an honorary title for a great musician.   _____

Score: _____ points

This 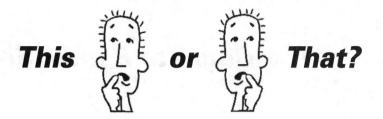 or That?

Circle the right word for each of these sentences.

1. Ralph is my **oldest / mayor** son.

2. She plans on being a nuclear **scientific / scientist** when she grows up.

3. Do you ever read the **editorials / publishing houses** in this magazine?
   They're usually very good and very controversial.

4. Today all successful writers have **publishers / editors** who check their work and give
   them suggestions.

5. Do you know who Abraham Lincoln's **murderer / assassin** was?

6. Just by **casualty / accident** I met my English teacher at the supermarket.

7. Little children don't always like to share things. They're sometimes **selfish / egoist**.

8. Every one of my aunts, uncles, and cousins will be at my wedding. I'm so happy that
   all my **relations / parents** will be there!

9. Do you know who the **director / conductor** of the London Philarmonic
   Orchestra is tonight?

10. Richard Stanley's new novel is so exciting! I hope his **publisher / editor** does a
    good job advertising the book all over the world.

The Cognate Repair Shop

Correct any vocabulary errors you find in the following sentences. Work on your own or with a partner.

1. How many scientifics will be at that international cancer conference?

2. I know that Henry and Carla are very close. What's their relation?

3. The musicians in this orchestra don't like their director's interpretations of Mozart.

4. When I was in high school, I was the publisher of our school newspaper.

5. I just re-read the biblical story of the assassination of Abel by his brother Cain.

6. "Are your parents coming to your graduation?"
   "Yes, all my aunts and uncles!"

7. Many people doubt that Lee Harvey Oswald was a lone murderer.

8. I got 90% on the test because I guessed. I chose the right answers by casualty.

9. "Can't I play with your toys, Billy?"
   "No! They're mine!"
   "You know, Billy, you shouldn't be so egoist."

10. I just found out that your brother is going to be a French maestro at our high school. Is that true?

Unit 2: Concrete Things

My Word!

antique   a piece of furniture or other object from the past that is considered valuable for nostalgic or aesthetic reasons

She worked as an antique dealer in the city's design district.

 NOTICE!

Don't confuse the English word *antique* with the Spanish word **antiguo**. In English, **antiguo** is *old*.

Let's throw out that couch. It's old and stained.

camp   1. a place where people decide to stop in the outdoors to spend the night

The hikers made camp next to a river.

2. a place where children go during the summer to participate in all kinds of activities with other children; they can go daily or live at the camp for the whole summer if they wish to

When I was a kid, my parents sent me to summer camp in the mountains every July and I'd stay there until the end of August.

 NOTICE!

In English, the Spanish word **campo** is:

1. *field:*
   a) a broad, level expanse of open land

   They decided to have their picnic in a field next to their farm.

b) an area of activity or knowledge

I'm in the medical field. I'm a radiologist.

2. *the country* (as opposed to the city)

We used to live in the city, but now we have a house in the country.

to camp to make camp

The girl scouts camped for the night at a lake in a beautiful valley.

carpet a soft, thick, comfortable floor covering

People who live in cold climates like to have carpets in every room of their houses.

 NOTICE!

1. In English, the Spanish word **carpeta** can be a *file folder* or simply *folder*.

We keep all our reports in those (file) folders and then put them in that file cabinet.

2. In English, **carpeta** can also be a *doily*, an ornamental piece of crochet work or lace.

My grandmother used to put doilies on her dining room table.

cart a vehicle with wheels that is pulled by a domestic animal or pushed by hand

In some rural areas, you still see people transported in ox carts.

In supermarkets, customers use shopping carts to hold all their groceries.

to cart   to move something by cart, wagon, and so forth

> You can still find places where things are carted by mules pulling wagons.

NOTICE!

In English, the Spanish word **carta** is *letter.*

> I just wrote a five-page letter to my friend in Cádiz, Spain.

carton   a container, like a box, for eggs, milk, and the like

> If you're going to the supermarket, please get a carton of eggs.

NOTICE!

In English, the Spanish word **cartón** is *cardboard.*

> Most food and other things are delivered to a supermarket in large cardboard boxes.

college   an institution of higher education; can be part of a university

> When our son and daughter graduated from high school, they both became college students.

NOTICE!

In English, the Spanish word **colegio** is *school,* usually meaning anywhere from kindergarten to the end of high school.

> Where did you go to school before entering college?

exit   the way to go out

> All public buildings must have signs placed at or near all exits so that people know where they can get out of the buildings.

NOTICE!

In English, the Spanish word **éxito** is *success.*

> We wish you success in your new business.

to exit   to go out

> During the fire drill, everybody exited the building as quickly as possible.

fabric   cloth, especially the cloth used in home decoration and clothing

> I really like the fabric you chose for the new living room drapes.

In English, the Spanish word **fábrica** is *factory*.

My son works in a factory that manufactures kitchen appliances.

fabrication   a lie; an invention of the imagination

That story he told us was a complete fabrication. I hope you didn't believe it.

horn   1. the hard, usually permanent structure growing on the heads of certain animals like cows

Some people in Asia think that a rhinoceros horn has medicinal powers.

2. the part of a car that makes a noise to warn other drivers or pedestrians

In some cities there are laws against motorists blowing their horns in residential areas.

3. a musical instrument

The horn section of a band or orchestra includes the tubas, trumpets, and trombones.

In English, the Spanish word **horno** is *oven*.

We bake bread in an oven.

hymn   a religious song usually written for and sung in a church

We will now sing Hymn No. 76.

In English, the Spanish phrase **himno nacional** is *national anthem*.

In the United States, the national anthem is played before baseball games begin.

library a place where you can go to borrow books or study

Many high school and college students like to study in a library because it's so quiet there.

NOTICE!

In English, the Spanish word **librería** is *bookstore*.

I'm going to the bookstore to buy the textbooks for my courses.

mark 1. the result (either a number or letter) that you have received on a test

Her marks have been so good that she should get an A in that course.

2. a stain

What's that mark on his collar? Oh! It's lipstick!

to mark 1. to review test papers, make corrections, and give a score (A, B, C; 100%, 90%, and so on)

We'll find out how we did on the test tomorrow; the teacher has finished marking the papers.

2. to make a visible impression

To distinguish his baggage from all the others, he marked his suitcases with bright red Xs.

NOTICE!

In English, the Spanish word **marca** can be *brand*.

Colgate is her favorite brand of toothpaste.

NOTICE!

In English, the Spanish word **marcar** is *to dial* (on a rotary telephone) and *to press* (on a touch-tone telephone).

If you don't dial a telephone number carefully, you'll get a wrong number.

If you have a touch-tone phone and wish to speak to an operator, please press 0 now.

mascara   a cosmetic used to color the eyelashes

Her eyes always look so big when she applies mascara.

NOTICE!

In English, the Spanish word **máscara** is *mask*.

On Halloween, children like to wear scary costumes and masks.

media   collective word for modes of communication: newspapers, magazines, television, and radio

Note: The word *media* is a plural noun in English, not singular.

People say that the media pay too much attention to scandal and not enough attention to really important news stories.

NOTICE!

In English, the Spanish word **media** can be *sock* or *stocking*.

She can't find one of her yellow socks.

note   1. a brief written message

Please give her this note when she returns.

2. a musical tone

That note is called 'doh' in some countries and the letter 'c' in others.

NOTICE!

In English, the Spanish word **nota** is *mark*, *grade*, or *score*.

What was your mark on the last test we had?

to note   to observe or perceive

She noted that he looked very tired even though he had slept for nine hours.

parade   a public procession on a ceremonial or festive occasion

On the American holiday called Thanksgiving, there is always a large parade along the street called Broadway in New York City.

NOTICE!

In English, the Spanish word **parada** is *stop*.

Is this the bus stop for the bus that goes downtown?

to parade   to march in or as if in a parade

The band members paraded around the field in their new uniforms.

patio   a recreational area, usually paved, next to or behind a house

We always cook out on our patio in the summer.

NOTICE!

The Spanish word **patio** can be *backyard* in American English and *garden* in British English.

We've planted different kinds of fruit trees in our backyard.

soap   The Spanish word for *soap* is **jabón**.

I just bought a wonderful bath soap that smells like roses.

NOTICE!

In English, the Spanish word **sopa** is *soup*.

My favorite soup is tomato soup. I think it's delicious.

tomb   a kind of chamber for the dead (pronounced "toom")

The ancient Egyptians buried their royalty in elaborate tombs.

NOTICE!

In English, the Spanish word **tumba** is *grave*.

There are hundreds of graves in that cemetery.

wagon   a four-wheeled vehicle usually pulled by a horse

Americans moved West in the 1800's in covered wagons.

Note: *Wagon* can also be a child's toy; in that case, it is pulled by the child.

Bobby put his baby brother in his little red wagon and pulled it all around the backyard.

NOTICE!

In English, the Spanish word **vagón** is *(railroad) car*.

Look how long that train is! It must have a hundred cars.

It's Under Construction

media	fabric
antique	soap
college	parades
library	mark
cart	patio
cartons	wagon
mascara	note
carpet	tomb
exit	hymn

Choose any two-word block. Write a sentence using both words. Write in pencil or erasable ink. Then choose another block and write another sentence. Keep going until you've used up all nine blocks.

1. _____

2. _____

3. _____

4. _____

5. _____

6. _____

7. _____

8. _____

9. _____

If you are in a class, exchange books with a partner. Read his/her sentences and let him/her read yours. If either of you finds any errors, discuss them and make any necessary corrections.

As I Was Saying...

Complete the following mini-conversations by using the list of vocabulary words for this unit. Each conversation has two speakers, Person A and Person B.

antique	carpet	fabric	library	media
camp	carton	hymns	mark	note

1. A: Are you going to the supermarket today?

    B: You want me to pick you up a _____ of eggs, right?

2. A: How old is that chair?

    B: One hundred years. It's a real _____.

    A: That's true. And it's amazing that the _____ on the seat is still in such wonderful condition.

3. A: Where are you going?

    B: To the _____ to look up some information and study. Want to come along?

4. A: You know, the wood floor in this room looks awful. It's all scratched.

    B: You're right. I guess we should put in a nice _____.

5. A: I just got back my algebra exam. I got an A on it! I can't believe it!

    B: You've never gotten such a high _____ in that class. Congratulations!

6. A: Have you heard the latest political scandal in Washington over Senator Harm?

    B: Of course. There's nothing else in the _____.

    A: The newspaper reporters are really attacking him.

    B: If I were the senator, I'd go to church and sing a lot of _____.

7. A: What are you doing with your children this summer?

    B: We're sending our kids to _____. They'll have a great time.

8. A: Do you know what the last _____ on the musical scale is?

    B: I'm not sure, but I think it's "ti" in some countries and "b" in others.

ALTA BOOK
CENTER
PUBLISHERS ID

14 Adrian Court
Burlingame
California, 94010
USA

Luis Quintero

Let's I.D. Them!

Do you remember this identification exercise? Work alone or with a partner. The exercise is on this and the next page. If you work with a partner, one of you has this page and the other one will work with the next page. Choose your page. Now get started.

Here's what to do if you work with a partner. If not, just write in your answers on both pages.

- Read No. 1 to your partner and write down his/her I.D. on the line provided.

- Then your partner will read No. 2 to you. You make the I.D. and he/she will write it down just as you did.

- Now read No. 3 and keep working this way until you're all done. Wait for your teacher to review the correct answers and then score your partner's answers.

Each answer = 10 points.

Exercise A

I.D.

1. It's the way out of a building. _____

3. You use this to wash or bathe. _____

5. You'll hear these sung in church. _____

7. You'll have this if you touch your pen point to your shirt. _____

9. This is a place you make in the woods to stay the night. _____

11. Milk can come in this kind of container. _____

13. This could be silk, cotton, or polyester. _____

15. This is where you go to school after high school. _____

17. This covers a floor. _____

19. This has four wheels and a horse or ox can pull it. _____

Score: _____ **points**

Read the instructions on the previous page and you'll know what to do. Remember, when you score your partner's answers or your own, each one = 10 points.

Exercise B   **I.D.**

2. My grandfather's pocket watch is one.   _____

4. It's where you can borrow books.   _____

6. In the U.S., this word often means university.   _____

8. It's next to your house and where you can cook out.   _____

10. This is where you can buy books.   _____

12. This word includes radio, TV, newpapers, and magazines. _____

14. Boxes that food comes in are made of this material.   _____

16. This is a place where things are manufactured.   _____

18. When people are in this, they march.   _____

20. This has wheels and you use it to move things around.   _____

                                    Score: _____ **points**

 **Face to Face**

Part A

Work alone or with a partner. Use this and the next page. If you work with somebody, decide who will look only at this page and who will look only at the next one.

By yourself: Read number 1 and then choose the best response from the next page. Continue through number 5, then start with number 6 on the next page and choose the response from this page.

With a partner: Read number 1 to your partner and he/she will select the best response from the other page. Continue until number 6. Now reverse how you do the exercise.

1. I like this mascara very much, don't you?

2. Where did you buy that book about vampires?

3. I have too many books in my house. I should store some in my garage.

4. What's your favorite soap?

5. Aren't tombs fascinating?

---

6. a) Okay, let's see the ones at the National Museum.

   b) Okay, let's see the ones in that shop at the mall.

   c) Okay, let's visit my relatives.

7. a) I think so, too. I wish it would go away.

   b) I think so, too. I wish it weren't in this neighborhood.

   c) I think so, too. I wish we had a different couch.

8. a) Cardboard.

   b) Crayon.

   c) Carton.

9. a) Sure, it's Sony.

   b) Sure, it's ink.

   c) Sure, it's expensive.

10. a) Yes. She wrote that she wants to see me.

    b) Yes. I got a B+.

    c) Yes. She is a very nice person.

Face to Face

Part B

1. a) Yes, this tailor really knows how to make clothes.

   b) Yes, it makes your eyelashes look very long.

   c) Yes, this factory makes excellent products.

2. a) In the bookstore on Biscayne Boulevard.

   b) In the library on Biscayne Boulevard.

   c) In the editorial at school.

3. a) Why don't you donate them to your school bookstore?

   b) Why don't you donate them to your school library?

   c) Why don't you sell them to your school editors?

4. a) Tomato.

   b) Budweiser.

   c) Palmolive.

5. a) Yes, especially the modern ones.

   b) Yes, especially the early 20th century English ones.

   c) Yes, especially the Egyptian and Mayan ones.

---

6. Feel like looking at antiques today?

7. That fabric is so ugly!

8. What's that shoe box made of?

9. Do you know what that mark is?

10. Did you get the note from your English teacher?

Unit 3: Abstract Things

My Word!

actually   really; to tell the truth; in fact

> "I didn't like the movie at all. Did you?"
> "Actually, I thought it was pretty good."

NOTICE!

In English, the Spanish word **actualmente** is *now* or *currently*. Also, the Spanish adjective **actual** is *current* or *present* in English.

> Currently, I'm taking a course in medieval history.

> The government says they will find a solution for the present economic crisis.

compromise   an agreement that is reached when originally each person wants something different

> She wanted to have Italian food, but I didn't. I wanted to have Indian food, but she didn't. We both like French food, so that's what we ate! We reached a compromise.

NOTICE!

1. In English, the Spanish word **compromiso** is commonly used to mean *engagement*, when two people have promised to marry each other. The couple *gets engaged*.

> They had a long engagement. It lasted for eight months.

2. **Compromiso** can also mean an *appointment* in English.

She had an appointment to get her hair cut at 3 o'clock.

to compromise   to reach an agreement

They compromised and decided to have French food that night.

crime   an act which goes against the law

Any time you break the law, you're committing a crime, even though some crimes are more serious, of course, than others.

NOTICE!

The Spanish words **crimen** and **criminal** can be stronger than the words *crime* and *criminal* in English. In certain cases, you would say that **crimen** is *murder* in English, and the person who does this, **el criminal**, is a *murderer*.

criminal   a person who has committed serious crimes, usually considered someone who does this habitually

Al Capone was one of the most notorious criminals in U.S. history. The crimes he committed included the illegal sale of alcohol and tax evasion.

disgrace   loss of honor, respect, or reputation

It was a great disgrace for his whole family when the police caught the teenager stealing from the neighbors.

NOTICE!

In English, the Spanish word **desgracia** is *misfortune* or *bad luck*.

He has nothing but bad luck every time he tries to open a business.

to disgrace   to bring shame or dishonor to somebody

The teenager disgraced his whole family when the police caught him stealing from the neighbors.

disgraceful   bringing shame, dishonor, or loss of respect

The way he acted during that formal dinner, making noise when he ate his soup and belching, was disgraceful. I was completely humiliated.

direction   1. the way something is going (north, south, east, west)

Columbus believed the right direction to sail to find India was west.

2. In the plural, *directions* means a series of instructions telling how to do something.

   If you follow my directions, you should find my house easily.

NOTICE!

In English, a common use of the Spanish word **dirección** is *address*.

   Please write your name, address, and phone number on this card.

education   what you learn in school

   Some people think you can get a better education in private schools than in public schools.

to educate   to teach somebody

   In the United States, some parents who don't like public schools choose to educate their children at home.

NOTICE!

In English, a common use of the Spanish word **educación** is *upbringing*, from the two-word verb to *bring up* when talking about what a family teaches their children at home.

   Parents have to be very wise to bring children up well.
   He's so polite because he had a good upbringing.

etiquette   the practices and forms prescribed by society or culture; good manners

   It's proper etiquette to wipe your mouth with a napkin while eating, and not with your sleeve or hand.

NOTICE!

In English, the Spanish word **etiqueta** can be *label*.

   I always check the label on a shirt or blouse to see how it should be washed.

frontier   the unexplored or unestablished part of a country; new territory

> In the 19th century, the West was the frontier for Americans and Canadians.

 NOTICE!

In English, the Spanish word **frontera** is *border*.

> When you come to the border, you'll have to show your passport.

propaganda   political ideas, information, and advertising to make people believe some doctrine

> During the Cold War, the Russians and the Americans bombarded each other with propaganda to make people think their ideas were the right ones.

 NOTICE!

In English, the Spanish word **propaganda** can be *advertising* when used in reference to commercials or written ads.

> If you want the public to buy your product, you'll need some clever advertising on television and radio. You should also advertise in magazines and newspapers.

ultimate   the greatest extreme, maximum

> Her ultimate dream is to become the head of the whole department.

 NOTICE!

In English, the Spanish word **último** is *last,* without the special meaning that *ultimate* has.

> The last time I saw Nilda was on Tuesday.

ultimately   finally; at the end

> Right now she's a salesperson. Ultimately she wants to become head of the whole department.

In English, the Spanish word **últimamente** commonly means *lately* or *recently*.

> Have you seen Nilda lately?

Going  Blank

Here is a list of the words you have just learned. Use them in the blanks that follow. Don't use a word more than once. Enjoy.

actually	*criminal*	*direction*	*etiquette*	*propaganda*
compromise	*disgrace*	*education*	*frontiers*	*ultimately*

1. If you're in Mexico City and you want to fly non-stop to San Francisco, which _____ are you going to fly in?

2. The United Nations has stopped many wars from happening because they were able to get the countries involved to reach a _____.

3. Peter lives close to my house. He _____ lives only two blocks away.

4. There are two kinds of courts in most countries, civil and _____.

5. According to the rules of _____, you should never make noises while you eat.

6. She worked hard to get a good _____. She now has two degrees from Yale University.

7. When there are so many people starving in the world, it's a _____ when other people waste food or just throw it out.

8. Nowadays the two _____ we have are the deep oceans and outer space.

9. We hope that there will be a colony on the moon in the 21st century. However, _____ we hope to colonize Mars and other planets, too.

10. One country claiming to be better than another is pure _____.

ALTA BOOK
CENTER
PUBLISHERS ID

14 Adrian Court
Burlingame
California, 94010
USA

Luis Quintero

Let's I.D. Them!

Do you remember this exercise? Work alone or with a partner. The exercise is on this and the next page. If you work with a partner, one of you has this page and the other one will work with the next page. Choose your page. Now let's get started.

Here's what to do if you work with a partner. If not, just write in your answers on both pages.

- Read No. 1 to your partner and write down his/her I.D. on the line provided.
- Then your partner will read No. 2 to you. You make the I.D. and he/she will write it down just as you did.
- Now you read No. 3 and keep working this way until you're all done. Wait for your teacher to review the correct answers and then score your partner's answers.

Each answer = 10 points.

Exercise 1-A   I.D.

1. This is the period between the time that two people   _____
   promise to get married and the day of the wedding.

3. This means unexplored territory.   _____

5. This word means "really."   _____

7. He has no manners. He had a bad . . .   _____

9. If you don't pay your taxes, it's a . . .   _____

Exercise 2-A   I.D.

1. This is when both people can agree on something.   _____

3. When he was caught stealing from his company,   _____
   he was in . . .

5. Never pick up food with a knife if you have this training.   _____

7. This thing on my shirt says it's made of 100% cotton.   _____

9. 3660 Biscayne Boulevard is my . . .   _____

Score: _____ points

Read the instructions on the previous page and you'll know what to do. Remember, when you score your partner's answers or your own, each one = 10 points.

Exercise 1-B   **I.D.**

2. This is another word in English for "real."   _____

4. Because it's the maximum, outer space is the _____ frontier. _____

6. Thieves, drug dealers, and murderers are _____.   _____

8. You receive this by going to school.   _____

10. Governments use this to make you believe their ideas.   _____

Exercise 2-B   **I.D.**

2. This means to raise a child.   _____

4. If you kill a person deliberately, it's called _____.   _____

6. This means the geographic, political line
   between two countries.   _____

8. This is another word for bad luck.   _____

10. North, south, east, and west are all _____
    on the compass.   _____

Score: _____ points

This  or That?

Circle the right word for each of these sentences.

1. **Propaganda / Advertising** on television can be very expensive.

2. His **education / upbringing** wasn't very good. That's why he's so impolite.

3. Not taking care of elderly parents is a **misfortune / disgrace**.

4. "How are your classes?" "My **current / actual** classes aren't too bad."

5. When we reach the **border / frontier**, will they ask us what our nationality is?

6. **Ultimately / Lately** I've been having severe headaches.

7. **Ultimately / Lately** I would like to retire without having to pay a mortgage.

8. Please write your **address / direction** here on this line of the application form.

9. In some states of the U.S., a convicted **criminal / murderer** gets a death sentence.

10. Remember, the **label / etiquette** says to dry clean this sweater only.

The Cognate Repair Shop

Correct any vocabulary errors you find in the following sentences. Work on your own or with a partner.

1. Is your actual address temporary?

2. Ana and Pablo have been compromised for three months.

3. If you have a good education, you don't belch in front of people.

4. Everything that company says is false propaganda if you ask me!

5. Do you think all criminals should get a death sentence or life in prison?

6. How many frontiers does your country have?

7. It was such a disgrace when their house burned down.

8. Ultimately I saw a friend of mine who I hadn't seen for three or four years.

9. I don't know what this dress is made of. The etiquette is missing.

10. I can't believe how much advertising your government sends out to other countries.

Unit 4: Conditions and States of Being

My Word!

appreciation   valuing something or somebody very much; being thankful

He has a great deal of appreciation for everything you've done.

 NOTICE!

In English, the Spanish word **apreciación** can mean your *opinion* or *feelings* about something.

Have I ever told you my feelings on that subject? I don't like it!

to appreciate   to recognize the value of something or somebody

I appreciate the things I have because I know so many people have less than I do.

balance   equilibrium

When people drink too much, they can lose their balance.

 NOTICE!

In English, the Spanish word **balanza** can be *scale*.

She got on her bathroom scale to see how much she weighed.

to balance   to have something in equilibrium

A sea lion can learn to balance a large ball on the tip of its nose.

complexion   the natural color and appearance of the skin, especially of the face

Her complexion is so beautiful that she doesn't need make-up.

 NOTICE!

In English, the Spanish word **complexión** is *constitution*, meaning a person's general physical condition and health.

At 90 years of age, her father was very proud of his strong constitution.

constipation   difficult or infrequent movement of the bowels

When you have constipation, you should take a laxative or drink prune juice to help you.

to be constipated   not able to go to the bathroom

You don't feel good when you are constipated.

 NOTICE!

In English, the Spanish phrase **estar constipado** can mean *to have a cold*.

My head hurts, I can't breathe through my nose, and I'm coughing a lot. I have a terrible cold.

disgust   a feeling of repugnance

He will never be a good fisherman because he always feels disgust at the sight of worms!

to disgust   to make somebody feel sick or offended

All the trash in their backyard disgusts me.

NOTICE!

In English, the Spanish word **disgustar** is *to displease*, and the noun, **disgusto**, is *displeasure*.

> It displeased me when nobody at customer service in that department store knew how to help me.

disgusted   feeling sick, repulsed, or very annoyed

> When he failed his driver's license test for the third time, he felt disgusted.

gusto   vigorous enjoyment

> Everything he does, he does with gusto. He really knows how to enjoy life!

 NOTICE!

In English, the Spanish word **gusto** means *taste, flavor,* or *pleasure*. But when it's used to mean *pleasure,* it's not as strong in meaning as the English word.

> I don't like the taste of this meat. I think it was too old when you cooked it.

> "It's very nice to meet you."
> "The pleasure is all mine."

injury   a wound or other specific damage to the body

> They received minor injuries in the automobile accident.

 NOTICE!

In English, the Spanish word **injuria** is *insult* or *offense*.

> It's an offense to all civilized people to see an animal abused.

to injure   to give somebody an injury

The train crash injured many passengers.

Note: In English, there is also the word *to damage* (a verb), *damage* (a noun), and *damaged* (an adjective). Usually, *damage* refers to things, not people. We use *to injure, injury,* and *injured* for people.

His car was damaged a lot in the accident.

In English, the Spanish word **injuriar** is *to offend* or *insult.*

That ethnic joke you told really offends me.

insanity   a serious mental disorder

In the novel *King's Row,* a doctor commits suicide because he thinks insanity runs in his family and that he will be the next to suffer from it.

insane   really crazy

The insane man started shooting people on the street.

NOTICE!

In English, the Spanish phrase **no está sano** is *he/she is unhealthy* or *he/she isn't healthy* (in the physical sense). The word *sane* always refers to *mental health* in English, so if you say somebody is not sane or he/she is insane, you mean he/she is crazy. (See *sane* further on in this unit.)

She was unhealthy as a child, but now she has a robust constitution.

inversion   the act of turning something inside out or upside down

Some plants grow well only if there is an inversion. For example, when you plant a piece of papyrus, you cut off a piece, put the top of the cut piece down into the ground and the bottom of the piece up.

NOTICE!

In English, the Spanish word **inversión** can be *investment* when speaking about money. The Spanish word **invertir** is *to invest* in English.

> His investment in AT&T has grown and is worth five times what he originally paid for the stock. He invested very wisely.

jubilation   a joyful celebration; exultation

> When the astronauts landed on the moon in 1969, Americans expressed great jubilation.

 NOTICE!

In English, the Spanish word **jubilación** can mean *retirement* or *pension*.

> They've made wonderful plans for their retirement years. With the nice pension they'll be getting every month, they will have enough money to travel a lot and spend more time with their children and grandchildren.

jubilant   extremely happy

> Everyone felt jubilant over the wonderful news.

mutilation   disfiguration or serious damage (normally done to a part of the body)

> Some insane people have done self-mutilation.

to mutilate   to disfigure or seriously damage a part of something

> When the bear attacked the camper, it mutilated his left arm.

 NOTICE!

The Spanish word **mutilar** can have the English meaning, but it also means to lose a limb or other body part because of an accident or amputation.

mutilated   having some kind of mutilation

> In China a long time ago, women were mutilated for beauty. Their feet were incredibly small because, when they were children, their feet were wrapped up tightly and not allowed to grow normally.

preoccupation   the act of completely occupying somebody's mind or attention

> Her preoccupation with her daughter's wedding is making her forget to do everyday chores.

In English, the Spanish word **preocupación** is *worry*.

Worry can give a person so much stress that it can cause a heart problem.

to be preoccupied   to be mentally occupied completely by one thing so that you forget many other important things

They're so preoccupied with their vacation plans that they forgot to find somebody to take care of their dog while they're away.

sanity   mental health

To keep our sanity, we take a few short vacations during the year.

In English, the Spanish word **sanidad** is *healthiness* or *sanitation*.

To maintain healthiness, you should eat properly and exercise.

For reasons of sanitation, cities collect residents' garbage.

sane   mentally healthy

Living in a nice house in a quiet area of the suburbs keeps her sane.

sympathy   a feeling or expression of sadness for another person who has suffered some terrible situation like a death in the family, losing a job, and so on

I know how hard it is to lose a parent. You have my sympathy.

With Deepest Sympathy...

In English, the Spanish word **simpatía** is *friendliness* or *affection*.

Everybody likes her because of her friendliness.

In English, the Spanish word **simpático** is *nice* or *friendly*.

We all like you very much. You're a very nice person.

to sympathize (with)   to have sympathy for somebody

I heard that you had the flu. I can sympathize with you; I had it, too.

success   achieving what you wanted to do

His company has had great success. They now have factories in many cities.

In English, the Spanish word **suceso** is *event*.

She watches the news on TV every day to keep up with current events.

In English, the Spanish word **suceder** is *to happen*.

Can you explain what happened when you arrived there?

It's Under Construction

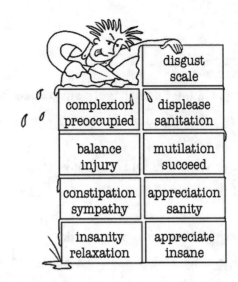

	disgust / scale
complexion / preoccupied	displease / sanitation
balance / injury	mutilation / succeed
constipation / sympathy	appreciation / sanity
insanity / relaxation	appreciate / insane

Choose any two-word block. Write a sentence using both words. Write in pencil or erasable ink. Then choose another block and write another sentence. Keep going until you've used up all nine blocks.

1. _____

2. _____

3. _____

4. _____

5. _____

6. _____

7. _____

8. _____

9. _____

If you are in a class, exchange books with a partner. Read his/her sentences and let him/her read yours. If either of you finds any errors, discuss them and make any necessary corrections.

 **As I Was Saying . . .**

Complete the following mini-conversations by using the list of vocabulary words for this unit. Each conversation has two speakers, Person A and Person B.

appreciation	constipation	injuries	jubilation	sanity
balance	disgusts	invested	preoccupied	sympathy
complexion		investment		success

1. A: How do you keep your _____ so beautiful and healthy looking?

   B: Oh, that's easy. I use this moisturizing cream every night on my face.

2. A: Why can't you ride a bicycle?

   B: I have a terrible sense of _____ .

3. A: I have a good marriage, two fine kids, and a good job.

   B: Do you consider yourself a _____?

   A: I certainly do.

4. A: To show our _____ for your 25 years of service to the company, we would like to present you with this gold watch.

   B: Thank you.

5. A: How do you keep your _____ when you work in this noisy office?

   B: By living outside the city and escaping at five o'clock every day!

6. A: I need a laxative.

   B: Why? Are you suffering from _____ again?

   A: I'm afraid I am.

   B: You have all my _____. I know how awful it makes you feel.

7. A: Did she suffer any serious _____ in the accident?

   B: No, I'm happy to say. She just had a few minor cuts and bruises.

8. A: I could never be an emergency room doctor or nurse.

   B: How come?

   A: The sight of blood _____ me. I really feel sick when I see injured people.

9. A: I'm feeling so happy!

   B: Why? What's up?

   A: My son's won a scholarship to medical school. He's been _____ with it for months and has thought of almost nothing else.

   B: Well, I guess there's _____ in this house. Lots of celebrating, right?

   A: Oh, I'm going to plan a big party to celebrate his getting the scholarship.

10. A: How's the stock market doing these days?

   B: Not too badly, actually. I _____ in a small company last year that makes computer parts. The stock has tripled since I bought it.

   A: Wow! That was definitely a good _____.

ALTA BOOK
CENTER
PUBLISHERS ID

14 Adrian Court
Burlingame
California, 94010
USA

Luis Quintero

Let's I.D. Them!

Work alone or with a partner. The exercise is on this and the next page. If you work with a partner, one of you has this page and the other one will work with the next page. Choose your page. Now get started.

Here's what to do if you work with a partner. If not, just write in your answers on both pages.

- Read No. 1 to your partner and write down his/her I.D. on the line provided.

- Then your partner will read No. 2 to you. You make the I.D. and he/she will write it down just as you did.

- Now read No. 3 and keep working this way until you're all done. Wait for your teacher to review the correct answers and then score your partner's answers.

Each answer = 10 points.

Exercise A

                                               I.D.

1. If you do things with energy and joy, you do them with this. _____

3. You use this to weigh yourself or something else. _____

5. When you put money into the stock market, you do this. _____

7. This is a cut or a broken bone. _____

9. When you're healthy and strong, you have a good _____. _____

11. This is when one thing takes all your mental energy. _____

13. Saying your mother looks like a horse is one of these. _____

15. To ride a bicycle, you have to have a good sense of _____. _____

17. This is the opposite of crazy. _____

19. For some, this is having enough money or material things. _____

Score: _____ **points**

Read the instructions on the previous page and you'll know what to do. Remember, when you score your partner's answers or your own, each one = 10 points.

Exercise B   **I.D.**

2. If you feel bad about another person's trouble, you can _____. _____

4. This is when you value what someone did.   _____

6. This is the color and look of a person's facial skin.   _____

8. He hasn't gone to the bathroom in three days.   _____

   He must be _____.

10. People who suffer from this are put in mental hospitals.   _____

12. He was _____ when he found a worm in the apple he was eating. _____

14. You have this if you have no mental disease.   _____

16. When something important happens, it's called a special   _____

    _____.

18. When his father passed away, I sent him a _____ card.   _____

20. Vincent Van Gogh did this to himself by cutting off his ear. _____

Score: _____ **points**

 **Face to Face**

Part A

Work alone or with a partner. Use this and the next page. If you work with somebody, decide who will look only at this page and who will look only at the next one.

By yourself: Read number 1 and then choose the best response from the next page. Continue through number 5, then start with number 6 on the next page and choose the response from this page.

With a partner: Read number 1 to your partner and he/she will select the best response from the other page. Continue until number 6. Now reverse how you do the exercise.

1. You have what we call in English a "peaches and cream" complexion.

2. How did she get that injury?

3. I can't believe I'm constipated again.

4. How do you appreciate something?

5. Isn't he a very sympathetic person?

---

6. a) Of course. Who wants to see the world through crazy eyes?

   b) Of course. It's the only way to stop having pests in your house and germs, too.

   c) Of course. We need it to keep prices down.

7. a) Appreciation.

   b) Appraisal.

   c) Approximation.

8. a) Sure, I do. I get on the doctor's office once a month.

   b) Sure, I do. I get on the balance once a month.

   c) Sure, I do. I get on the scale once a month.

9. a) Yes. In fact, the injury was terrible.

   b) Yes. In fact, the damage was terrible.

   c) Yes. In fact, the destroyed was horrible.

10. a) They declared he had insanity when he attacked that man and killed him.

    b) They declared he was sane when he attacked that man and killed him.

    c) They declared he was insane when he attacked that man and killed him.

Face to Face

Part B

1. a) That's a wonderful dessert.

   b) Thank you. That sounds like a compliment.

   c) It's because I work out in a gym four times a week.

2. a) When her neighbor told her that she had no morals.

   b) When a car crashed into the fence in front of her house.

   c) When she was skiing in Vermont.

3. a) Why don't you eat prunes? They'll help stop that.

   b) Why don't you take some tea with lemon and honey? You'll feel better.

   c) Why don't you go to the emergency room?

4. a) By looking at the receipt.

   b) By understanding how important it is to you.

   c) By taking it to an expert.

5. a) Yes, he's always so nice.

   b) Yes, he always understands your problems and gives good advice.

   c) Yes, he sends beautiful cards.

---

6. Sanity is very important, isn't it?

7. What's something you want from family and friends?

8. You have such a nice figure. I bet you never need to weigh yourself.

9. Did you have lots of destruction from the hurricane?

10. How is it that the jury didn't find him guilty of first-degree murder?

Unit 5A: Words that Describe

My Word!

ancient   something very old, usually going back over one thousand years

Archaeologists are fascinated by the ancient civilizations of Egypt, Rome, and Greece.

NOTICE!

In English, the Spanish word **anciano** is simply *old*.

He's getting old now. He's in his 70's.

brave   full of courage; not afraid of things

The brave soldiers were given medals for their heroic deeds.

NOTICE!

In English, the Spanish word **bravo** can be *angry*.

Don't get so angry with me every time I make a mistake!

bravery   the act of being brave

Their bravery was so impressive that the general gave them medals.

content   satisfied

I know I'll never be rich, but that's okay; I'm content with what I have.

NOTICE!

In English, the Spanish word **contento** is *happy*.

We were very happy when our daughter graduated from college.

contentment the state of being content

Our contentment with what we have keeps us from feeling envious of others.

delinquent 1. not doing what you are supposed to do

The boy was usually delinquent in doing his homework, which made his teacher very unhappy with him.

2. late in doing something

People who are delinquent in returning books to the library must pay a fine for each extra day they keep books out.

NOTICE!

In English, the Spanish word **delincuente** is *guilty* or *criminal* and has a much stronger meaning than the English word.

A juvenile delinquent is a young person who is always in trouble at school and maybe even with the police.

delinquency failure to do something

His delinquency in returning library books has cost him over $28.00 in fines this year.

embarrassed feeling uncomfortable, not at ease, usually because unwanted attention is on you

Marci was embarrassed to admit that she was secretly in love with Ron.

NOTICE!

In English, the Spanish word **embarazada** is *pregnant*.

Did you know that Ana is pregnant? She'll have the baby in May.

to embarrass   to make somebody feel uncomfortable or uneasy

> Marci's best friend Glenda embarrassed her when she told Ron that Marci was secretly in love with him.

embarrassing   describing the cause of the embarrassment

> It was very embarrassing for Marci when Glenda told Ron the truth.

fresh   1. recently made, produced, or harvested

> Nothing smells better than bread that's fresh from the oven.

2. not preserved by any means

> We only like to eat fresh vegetables, not canned or frozen ones.

In English, the Spanish word **fresco** can be *cool.*

> You know, it's getting cool outside. I think I'll put on a sweater.

freshness   the condition of being fresh

> You can tell the freshness of green beans by seeing if they snap easily in your hand when you bend them.

in front of   directly before another thing or person

> They just put a "for sale" sign in front of their house.

NOTICE!

In English, the Spanish phrase **en frente de** is often translated as "in front of" when it really should be translated as *across from* or *opposite.*

The post office is across from/opposite the bank on Main Street.

intoxicated   drunk; affected by immoderate consumption of alcoholic drinks

He was arrested by the police for driving while intoxicated.

NOTICE!

In English, the Spanish word **intoxicado** is *poisoned.*

They rushed the baby to the emergency room because they were sure she was poisoned by the paint she had put in her mouth.

to intoxicate   to make somebody (feel) drunk

Six glasses of beer will intoxicate practically anybody.

intoxicating   making someone (feel) drunk or dizzy

The smell of her perfume was intoxicating. Don't you agree?

Going  Blank

Here is a list of the words you have just learned. Use them in the blanks that follow. Don't use a word more than once. Enjoy.

ancient	content	embarrassed	in front of
brave	delinquent	fresh	intoxicated

1. The fact that the driver smelled of beer and couldn't walk straight proved that he was _____.

2. One of the most _____ civilizations in the Americas was the Maya.

3. Now, be a _____ little boy when the doctor gives you the injection.

4. The teacher seats her students alphabetically. I'm Joan Stoffer, so Amy Stewart sits _____ me.

5. Hello. Mr. Dunlop? This is the Acme Mortgage Company. I see that you've been _____ in paying your mortgage again. You are two payments late.

6. A: Don't you want to move up in the company?

   B: No, I'm _____ to stay where I am. I like this job.

7. A: Oh! Look at that man selling vegetables and fruit at the side of the road.

   B: I bet they're all very _____. Let's stop and buy some.

8. The parents became very _____ when their child started to cry in church during the service.

ALTA BOOK
CENTER
PUBLISHERS ID

14 Adrian Court
Burlingame
California, 94010
USA

Luis Quintero

Let's I.D. Them!

Work alone or with a partner. The exercise is on this and the next page. If you work with a partner, one of you has this page and the other one will work with the next page. Choose your page. Now get started.

Here's what to do if you work with a partner. If not, just write in your answers on both pages.

- Read No. 1 to your partner and write down his/her I.D. on the line provided.

- Then your partner will read No. 2 to you. You make the I.D. and he/she will write it down just as you did.

- Now you read No. 3 and keep working this way until you're all done. Wait for your teacher to review the correct answers and then score your partner's answers.

Each answer = 10 points.

Exercise 1-A   I.D.

1. It's the opposite of *behind*.   _____

3. When a person drinks too much, he gets like this. _____

5. It's the opposite of *innocent*.   _____

7. It's the opposite of *modern*.   _____

9. A coward is a person who isn't like this.   _____

Exercise 2-A   I.D.

1. It's the opposite of *new* or *young*.   _____

3. You can feel this way when you say the wrong thing. _____

5. If you accidentally swallow arsenic, you will be this way. _____

7. If you're late paying your bills, you're _____. _____

9. This coffee was made an hour ago. It isn't _____ anymore. _____

Score: _____ points

Read the instructions on the previous page and you'll know what to do. Remember, when you score your partner's answers, each one = 10 points.

Exercise 1-B   **I.D.**

2. If you're satisfied with something, you feel like this.   _____

4. People get medals of honor if they have this quality.   _____

6. Sometimes, the strong fragrance of flowers
   can make you feel this way.   _____

8. Your credit rating will be terrible if you show this bad quality
   whenever it's time to pay your bills.   _____

10. People who are this way aren't afraid.   _____

Exercise 2-B   **I.D.**

2. They have a porch facing the street. It's ____ their house.   _____

4. Day-old bread is no longer this way.   _____

6. You'll feel this way if your child uses vulgar words in front of
   your relatives or neighbors.   _____

8. This is how you could be if you eat unsafe, wild mushrooms.   _____

10. This is what we call something that is 2,000 years old.   _____

Score: _____ **points**

This 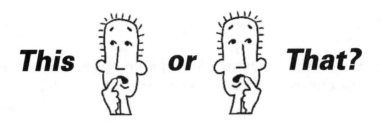 or That?

Circle the right word for each of these sentences.

1. Don't get **brave / angry** with me every time I talk about our problems.

2. I see you're **pregnant / embarrassed** again. What personal information did your husband give the neighbors this time?

3. You want the antique store? Do you know where the supermarket is? Okay, it's **in front of / across from** the supermarket. You can't miss it.

4. Your father's 92 years old? Incredible! I didn't know he was so **ancient / old**.

5. He can't keep a job because his bosses always find out that he was sent to jail for being **delinquent / criminal** on his child support payments.

6. I see you're **pregnant / embarrassed** again. Do you expect a boy or girl this time?

7. She left her husband because he was arrested again for being **poisoned / intoxicated** while driving.

8. Many **ancient / old** civilizations knew how to use a wide variety of plants as medicines.

9. You got a perfect score on the final exam? You must be very **content / happy**.

10. I like warm days and **fresh / cool** nights. How about you?

The Cognate Repair Shop

Correct any vocabulary errors you find in the following sentences. Work on your own or with a partner.

1. My house is the one in front of the drugstore.

2. When I exercise, I don't like to drink ice cold water; I just like it to be fresh.

3. Let's take the cat to the veterinarian. I think she ate a lizard and is intoxicated.

4. I don't want to talk about that subject anymore. Don't make me brave!

5. His guilty behavior caused him to drop out of high school.

6. A: Why are you so content?

   B: I just won the lottery!

7. Now that you know you're embarrassed, are you going to stop smoking?

8. This museum is full of old artifacts from Greece, Mycenae, and Crete.

Unit 5B: Words that Describe

My Word!

humid   describes air with a high content of moisture

The climate in the Amazon rain forest is very warm and humid.

 NOTICE!

The Spanish word **húmedo** can be used for things, not just the air. But in English, we use the adjective *damp* for things.

Note: The adjective *damp* normally has a negative connotation.

I can't take the clothes out of the dryer yet; they're still damp.

I don't like it when the weather is very humid and the carpets in our house feel damp.

Note: In English, the adjective is *moist* for certain foods like cake, for the lips, for the soil, etc. The adjective *moist* normally has a positive connotation.

This cake is wonderful. It's so moist. Every time I bake a cake, it comes out too dry. What's your secret?

I use this salve on my lips to keep them moist when the weather is cold and dry.

You don't have to water those flowers yet. The soil around them is still moist.

large   big

Their house is very large. It has six bedrooms!

 NOTICE!

In English, the Spanish word **largo** is *long.*

There's a very long tunnel that goes through that mountain.

nude   without any clothes

Michelangelo's famous statue of David is completely nude.

 NOTICE!

In English, the Spanish word **nudo** is *knot.*

She couldn't untie her shoe because there was a knot in the laces.

particular   separate and distinct; exceptional; individual; special

Even though they like all kinds of cheesecake, they have a particular liking for New York style cheesecake.

 NOTICE!

In English, the Spanish word **particular** can mean *private.*

They have hired a private teacher for their two children. The children are being educated at home instead of going to school.

personal   of a particular person; private

Don't open my mail! That's personal.

 NOTICE!

The English word *personal* never means all the employees of a company as it can mean in Spanish. In that case, we use the word *personnel* in English.

To apply for that job, please fill out an application form in the personnel department.

rare 1. unusual; hard to find; uncommon

Diamonds are so expensive because they're rare gemstones.

2. not cooked much

I like my steak rare.

In English, the Spanish word **raro** is *strange.*

It was really strange to see a purple cow!

sensible acting with or showing good sense; reasonable; intelligent

It's sensible to take an umbrella with you if you think it's going to rain.

In English, the Spanish word **sensible** is *sensitive.*

Because she has such a light complexion, her skin is very sensitive to the sun.

He's a very sensitive person. You can hurt his feelings very easily.

The opposite can be the word *insensitive.*

He does not care about other people's feelings. He is a very insensitive person.

unedited not corrected or changed by an editor

This is the original manuscript. It's still unedited.

In English, the Spanish word **inédito** is *unpublished.*

Can you imagine. Just a few years ago they found some unpublished music of Mozart's. What an incredible discovery!

vicious   cruel, malicious

> Those recent newspaper reports about the President were a vicious attack against his honor.

In English, the Spanish word **vicioso** can mean *addicted* to things like cigarettes, drugs, or alcohol.

> She is addicted to cigarettes. She smokes two packs a day.

It's Under Construction

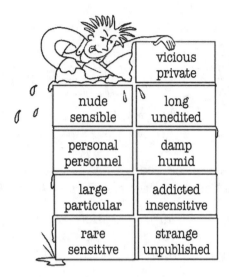

	vicious private
nude sensible	long unedited
personal personnel	damp humid
large particular	addicted insensitive
rare sensitive	strange unpublished

Choose any two-word block. Write a sentence using both words. Write in pencil or erasable ink. Then choose another block and write another sentence. Keep going until you've used up all nine blocks.

1. _____

2. _____

3. _____

4. _____

5. _____

6. _____

7. _____

8. _____

9. _____

If you are in a class, exchange books with a partner. Read his/her sentences and let him/her read yours. If either of you finds any errors, discuss them and make any necessary corrections.

As I Was Saying . . .

Complete the following mini-conversations by using the list of vocabulary words for this unit.
Each conversation has two speakers, Person A and Person B.

damp	large	particular	private	unedited
humid	long	personal	rare	unpublished
insensitive	moist	personnel	sensible	vicious
	nude		strange	

1. A: Why is my hair still so _____? I washed it hours ago.

    B: It's because the air is so _____ today.

2. A: An elephant is a very _____ animal, isn't it?

    B: It certainly is. And it has a very _____ nose, called a trunk.

3. A: Have you been to the beach on Virginia Island yet?

    B: No, I haven't. But isn't that _____ beach exclusively for _____
    sunbathing? I wouldn't feel comfortable there if I couldn't wear a bathing suit.

    A: I understand. Many people think that kind of sunbathing should be done in
    _____, not in public.

4. A: I wrote my first novel eight years ago, but it's still _____ because all the
    publishers say it's too controversial and they're afraid to publish it. The problem is
    they only saw the _____ version before all the changes were made.

    B: Try submitting the manuscript again to them and be more optimistic.

5. A: You know, there are some _____ people working in the _____
    department of this company. Have you seen the young woman with the orange hair?

    B: Yes, I have. Incredible! I saw her when I went to find out about the changes in our
    health insurance plan. To tell you the truth, I don't like it when people like that have
    easy access to _____ information about us.

A: I guess we should remember that old proverb which says "Don't judge a book by its cover."

B: You're probably right.

6. A: I hear that Professor Strei is going on safari again to the jungles of Central Africa to look for _____ plants that may contain cures for diseases.

B: Yes, he is. He's always looking for hard-to-find specimens. He's careful about traveling too. He always takes the most _____ routes and avoids using backroads.

A: Why does he take so many precautions?

B: Because he once was attacked by a/an _____ wild animal, and nearly lost his life. It was horrible. The animal sank its teeth into his arm and wouldn't let go for a long time. He was lucky not to get rabies.

A: Now I see why he takes no chances these days.

7. A: Why is my plant dying? I water it every day.

B: Ah! You probably water it too much. How _____ is the soil every day?

8. A: There was so much violence in that movie! How could you watch all of it?

B: I don't know. I guess I've seen so much violence on TV that I'm _____ to it; it doesn't affect me anymore.

ALTA BOOK
CENTER
PUBLISHERS ID

14 Adrian Court
Burlingame
California, 94010
USA

Luis Quintero

Let's I.D. Them!

Work alone or with a partner. The exercise is on this and the next page. If you work with a partner, one of you has this page and the other one will work with the next page. Choose your page. Now get started.

Here's what to do if you work with a partner. If not, just write in your answers on both pages.

- Read No. 1 to your partner and write down his/her I.D. on the line provided.
- Then your partner will read No. 2 to you. You make the I.D. and he/she will write it down just as you did.
- Now read No. 3 and keep working this way until you're all done. Wait for your teacher to review the correct answers and then score your partner's answers.

Each answer = 10 points.

Exercise 1-A   I.D.

1. If it rains a lot, the ground is usually like this.   _____

3. He's like this because he doesn't like telling details of his life. _____

5. After it rains on a hot day, the air is this way.   _____

7. A German shepherd is a dog of this size.   _____

9. You can tie two pieces of rope together by making this.   _____

Exercise 1-B   I.D.

1. This is another word for something really cruel.   _____

3. *Naked* is another word for this condition.   _____

5. If you're like this, you won't wear dress shoes on a hike.   _____

7. This conversation isn't for your ears. It's _____.   _____

9. Before publication, a book should always be _____.   _____

Score: _____ **points**

Read the instructions on the previous page and you'll know what to do. Remember, when you score your partner's answers or your own, each one = 10 points.

Exercise 2-A   **I.D.**

2. This collective word means all the employees.   _____

4. This word means the opposite of *normal.*   _____

6. When meat is not cooked much, we say it's this way.   _____

8. This person checks an author's work.   _____

10. This is the opposite of *sensitive.*   _____

Exercise 2-B   **I.D.**

2. You can make her cry very easily. She's much too _____.   _____

4. Colombian emeralds are expensive because   _____
   they're so hard to find. In other words, they're _____.

6. People like chocolate cake if it's this way and they don't   _____
   need to drink gallons of soda, coffee, or milk with it.

8. This word means *specific, special,* or *individual.*   _____

10. The boys were so _____ to the girl. They used to put worms   _____
    in her lunch.

Score: _____ **points**

 *Face to Face*

Part A

Work alone or with a partner. Use this and the next page. If you work with somebody, decide who will look only at this page and who will look only at the next one.

By yourself: Read number 1 and then choose the best response from the next page. Continue through number 5, then start with number 6 on the next page and choose the response from this page.

With a partner: Read number 1 to your partner and he/she will select the best response from the other page. Continue until number 6. Now reverse how you do the exercise.

1. I don't want the publishing company to change even one word of my work!

2. I wish you didn't stop talking to me every time we have a little argument.

3. I can tell that your dog, Max, was in the swimming pool earlier today.

4. Tell me something about your love life.

5. I know the room is 3 meters high and 4 meters wide.

_____

6. a) Thanks. I'm glad it didn't dry out; it's still humid.

   b) Thanks. I'm glad it didn't dry out; it's still moist.

   c) Thanks. I'm glad it didn't dry out; it's still damp.

7. a) No, I'm sorry. This is a particular driveway.

   b) No, I'm sorry. This is a personal driveway.

   c) No, I'm sorry. This is a private driveway.

8. a) That's because they're so strange.

   b) That's because they're so rare.

   c) That's because they're so yellow.

9. a) A sweater in the wintertime. Your gifts are always so sensible!

   b) A sweater in the wintertime. Your gifts are always so sensitive!

   c) A sweater in the wintertime. Your gifts are always so impractical!

10. a) Wasn't it editorialized in 1994?

    b) Wasn't it edited in 1994?

    c) Wasn't it published in 1994?

Face to Face

Part B

1. a) Can you really expect them to leave it edited?

   b) Can you really expect them to leave it unedited?

   c) Can you really expect them to edit so much?

2. a) I know I'm too angry.

   b) I know I'm too sensible.

   c) I know I'm too sensitive.

3. a) Oh, his hair must still be moist.

   b) Oh, his hair must still be humid.

   c) Oh, his hair must still be damp.

4. a) That's a personal issue.

   b) That's a personnel issue.

   c) I was born in Cleveland, Ohio, graduated from . . .

5. a) Okay, but how long is it?

   b) Okay, but how large is it?

   c) Okay, it seems big enough for our needs.

---

6. You baked the fish just right.

7. Can I park my car here?

8. Perfectly colored opals are such expensive gems, aren't they?

9. Here's your birthday present. Happy birthday!

10. Her first popular novel was wonderful. Have you read it?

Unit 6: Active Verbs

My Word!

to deceive   to give somebody the wrong information deliberately; to create a deception

> When he told his wife that she was the first woman he was serious about, he deceived her. Actually, he'd been married three times before.

deception/   the use of misrepresentation

deceit

> Not telling his wife that he'd been married before was a deception. When she found out the truth, she left him because of his deceit.

 NOTICE!

In English, the Spanish word **decepción** is *disappointment.*

> He thought seeing the pyramids of Egypt would be a romantic thing to do. It was a great disappointment to him when he found boys selling soda and candy all around the area.

to disappoint   to give somebody a disappointment

> The commercial atmosphere around the pyramids disappointed him.

demand   1. to ask for something very strongly; to insist

> The robber demanded that they give him all their money.

2. to require or need

> Brain surgery is very delicate work. It demands the surgeon's full concentration at all moments.

NOTICE!

In English, the Spanish word **demandar** can mean *to sue.*

> When the tree in my backyard fell onto his roof, he sued me for the repair costs.

discuss to have a conversation, to chat

> We discussed our vacation plans with a nice travel agent who gave us some useful advice.

NOTICE!

In English, the Spanish word **discutir** can be *to argue* and the noun, **discusión,** is *argument.*

> I argued that there should be more laws about owning guns, not fewer.

discussion a conversation

> Last Friday all the students in my conversation class had a discussion about the best way to look for a job.

doctor 1. to give medical treatment

> Without the help of a veterinarian, I doctored my parakeet as best I could.

2. to alter or falsify

> The thief doctored the stolen check by adding an extra zero so that $100 looked like $1000.

NOTICE!

In English, the Spanish word **doctorarse** is *to get a doctor's degree.*

> After so many years of study and hard work, she finally got her doctor's degree and can now get her license to practice medicine.

experiment the test to see if something is true or not

> Normally, researchers have to perform hundreds if not thousands of experiments to make any important discoveries or test a theory.

to experiment   to test whether or not something is true

> Researchers are experimenting with new drugs to see if they can destroy HIV, the virus that causes AIDS.

In English, the Spanish word **experimentar** can mean *to experience*. The past participle, **experimentado,** is used as the adjective, which in English is *experienced.*

> She's an experienced tour guide. She's taken literally hundreds of tour groups through the Vatican in the past few years.

explain   to make clear, plain, or comprehensible

> I like my teacher because she explains things to us so clearly.

In English, the Spanish word **explanar** is *to grade* or *to level.*

> When they prepared the foundation for our new house, they had to level the ground very carefully. Then they graded the patio area in the back to make sure the rain water would go away from the house, not towards it.

explanation   what is said to make something comprehensible

> She expected a big explanation from him for not coming home on time.

ignore   to refuse to pay attention to somebody or something

> "Doesn't that loud music from your neighbor's apartment bother you?"
> "No, I just ignore it; I don't even hear it half the time."

NOTICE!

In English, the Spanish word **ignorar** can be *not to know.*

> There are many things in this world that I don't know, but I'm always happy to learn something new.

ignorance   the condition of not knowing things

> We were in complete ignorance of the law; we thought we didn't need to wear seatbelts in the car all the time.

ignorant   being uneducated

> He knows absolutely nothing. He's the most ignorant person I've ever met.

Note: These two words *(ignorance; ignorant)*, especially the adjective, *ignorant*, are considered to be very strong words, which some people think are equal to insults.

introduce   to identify and make one person or thing known to others

> Jaime, I'd like to introduce you to my friend, Pedro.

NOTICE!

In English, the Spanish word **introducir** is *to insert* or *to put into.*

> The nurse inserted/put the intravenous needle into the patient's hand to prepare him for surgery.

introduction   the act of making one person or thing known to others

> Our next guest needs no introduction, ladies and gentlemen. You all know him from the many great movies he's starred in.

record   to write down or put on video or audio tape so that something will be remembered

> The first man in history to record his voice was Thomas Edison.

Note: The pronunciation between the verb, *to record*, and the noun, *a record*, changes dramatically. The verb is "ree - KORD," but the noun is "REH - kerd."

NOTICE!

In English, the Spanish word **recordar** is *to remember* or *to remind* (somebody).

I remember when I was a child, I always wanted to play in mud puddles.

This dish reminds me of my grandmother's cooking.

NOTICE!

In English, the Spanish word **recuerdo** is *memory* or *souvenir*. And in the plural form, **recuerdos** can mean *regards* in English.

We have such nice memories of our romantic vacation in Venice.

Tourists always like to buy souvenirs from the places they visit.

When you see your uncle, please give him my regards.

resolve
1. to make a firm decision or have a decision by a formal vote

The committee resolved to offer John Garner the job of treasurer.

2. to find a solution, an answer, normally used with the word *situation*

He tried to resolve the situation, but it only got worse.

NOTICE!

In English, the Spanish word ***resolver*** is usually translated with the verb *to solve*.

They solved their money problems when she got a part-time job.

Did the police ever solve the mystery of his disappearance?

resolution
the formal decision to do something

People make resolutions at New Year's to change the way they've done something in the past year.

reveal
to make known; to show clearly

The pirate revealed where he had buried the treasure.

NOTICE!

In English, the Spanish word **revelar** can be *to develop* when speaking of photographs.

I took three rolls of film to the camera shop to be developed.

revelation   when the truth comes out; when you recognize the truth

The revelation in the newspapers that the President was having an affair shocked everyone.

support   the maintenance in position; the provision of money, etc.

If you want to fight this case in court, I'll offer you all my moral support—and financial support as well!

to support   1. to maintain or hold in position

The old man supported himself with a cane when he walked.

2. to help somebody by giving money or approval

She supports her three kids by working two jobs.

Thanks for supporting my side in our political debate.

 NOTICE!

In English, the Spanish word **soportar** can be *to stand* or *to take* in the meaning of tolerate something or somebody.

I can't stand heavy metal music. My ears can't take it!

Going  Blank

Here is a list of the words you have just learned. Use them in the blanks that follow. Don't use a word more than once. Enjoy.

deception	*doctored*	*explain*	*records*	*solved*
demand	*experimented*	*ignored*	*resolve*	*souvenir*
discuss	*experienced*	*introduced*	*revealed*	*support*

1. A. How did he steal so much money from the company?

   B: He _____ the financial _____ so that nobody noticed the money was missing. His _____ fooled everybody.

2. I find algebra really confusing. Can you _____ this theorum again?

3. Before Columbus' time, there were no potatoes or tomatoes in Europe. It was the European explorers who _____ them to Europe in the 17th century.

4. Poor Joe. The doctor kept telling him to stop smoking, but he _____ the doctor's warnings and now he's very sick .

5. A: What happens to a monkey that's been _____ on for a long time?

   B: The scientists send it to a special kind of zoo where it's treated very well.

6. A: I'd like to _____ the rent increase with you.

   B: Fine. I think I should be getting more money for your apartment.

   A: Well, we don't. Is there any way we can _____ this situation?

   B: I'm afraid not. If you decide to move, that's fine with me. The _____ for apartments is very high right now, so I'll have no trouble getting new tenants.

7. A: Wow! You certainly hired Ms. Carlysle very quickly.

   B: She's very _____ . She's been an accountant for years.

8. It was _____ in today's newspaper that certain rich individuals are giving financial _____ to terrorist organizations. Isn't that horrible?

9. A: I really like this plate you have with the Pope's picture on it.

   B: So do I. It's a _____ I got when I visited the Vatican last summer.

10. A: Let me ask you something. You have a dog in your apartment, but you work all day, right?

    B: That's right.

    A: So how do you deal with the problem of walking your dog in the afternoon?

    B: I _____ the problem by hiring the kid next door to walk my dog when he comes home for lunch from school every day.

ALTA BOOK
CENTER
PUBLISHERS ID

14 Adrian Court
Burlingame
California, 94010
USA

Luis Quintero

Let's I.D. Them!

Work alone or with a partner. The exercise is on this and the next page. If you work with a partner, one of you has this page and the other one will work with the next page. Choose your page. Now get started.

Here's what to do if you work with a partner. If not, just write in your answers on both pages.

- Read No. 1 to your partner and write down his/her I.D. on the line provided.
- Then your partner will read No. 2 to you. You make the I.D. and he/she will write it down just as you did.
- Now read No. 3 and keep working this way until you're all done. Wait for your teacher to review the correct answers and then score your partner's answers.

Each answer = 10 points.

Exercise A   I.D.

1. It's a conversation.   _____

3. You can buy this at a tourist attraction.   _____

5. It means to put down in writing.   _____

7. It means to let the truth be known.   _____

9. When you let one person meet another for the first time.   _____

Exercise 2-A   I.D.

1. It's what you create when you lie to people.   _____

3. It means to try to find out if something will work or not.   _____

5. It means to provide money or food for some people.   _____

7. It means to pay no attention to somebody or something.   _____

9. It means to change or falsify something.   _____

Score: _____ **points**

Read the instructions on the previous page and you'll know what to do. Remember, when you score your partner's answers or your own, each one = 10 points.

Exercise 1-B   **I.D.**

2. It means to make somebody understand something.   _____

4. Working somewhere for a long time gives you this.   _____

6. It means to decide formally to do something.   _____

8. It's to misrepresent something so people believe the   _____
   wrong thing.

10. It means to insist very strongly.   _____

Exercise 2-B   **I.D.**

2. It's what you feel when you don't get what you expected.   _____

4. You do this when you go to court to get money from somebody. _____

6. This is what you do when you put a coin into a washing   _____
   machine at the laundromat.

8. It means to falsify or illegally change documents.   _____

10. This is the condition of knowing almost nothing.   _____

Score: _____ points

This  or That?

Circle the right word for each of these sentences.

1. Anthropologists try to **resolve / solve** mysteries about ancient humans.

2. That law firm has been in business for over thirty years. They have very
   experienced / experimented lawyers.

3. A: What are you going to do if that client refuses to pay you?

   B: I'm going to **sue / demand** him.

4. Look. It's 2 o'clock in the morning. I know we don't agree, but I don't want to
   discuss / argue with you at such a late hour. This can wait.

5. This job is so stressful. I can't **take / support** it anymore. I quit!

6. My kids were so sad when they found out the circus wasn't coming to town. What a
   disappointment / deception!

7. First you mix the sugar with the flour. Now you **introduce / put in** the eggs.

8. A: I don't think the problems in Russia are so terrible.

   B: You don't? You have the habit of **ignoring / not knowing** unpleasant events
   or situations. Things in Russia are really quite bad!

9. Did you **record / remember** to lock the front door on the way out?

10. I'd like to have all of these slides and photos **revealed / developed**.

The Cognate Repair Shop

Correct any vocabulary errors you find in the following sentences. Work on your own or with a partner.

1. I can't believe you recorded everything I'd said. What a memory you have!

2. Henry, I'd like to present you to my roommate, Carl.

3. I see that you ignore a lot about my country.

4. A: Why are they shouting like that?

   B: They're having a discussion about politics again.

5. Can you help me resolve this math problem?

6. What a deception! I thought I had finally won a prize. I really can't support it. I lost again!

7. The most experimented airline pilots are the ones who served in the military first.

8. When I cook a turkey or large beef roast, I always introduce a meat themometer so I can know the temperature of the meat accurately.

9. She was one of the best students at the medical school. She doctored in only three years when the average time is four.

10. I can't wait to reveal all these rolls of film from our vacation!

Unit 7: Acts

My Word!

apology   statement to say you are sorry for doing something wrong

I hope you accept my apology for the insults I shouted at you.

to apologize   to say you are sorry for doing something wrong

I'd like to apologize to you for those terrible things I said in anger.

 NOTICE!

In English, the Spanish word **apología** is *justification* or *defense* (among other things).

The teacher's justification for failing that student was that the student had missed too many classes.

The lawyer's defense of his client's actions was convincing.

assistance   help

Welcome to my shop. If you need any assistance, please don't hesitate to ask me.

to assist   to help

The young man assisted the lady by carrying her groceries from the supermarket to her car.

> **NOTICE!**
>
> In English, the Spanish word **asistencia** is *attendance* and the verb **asistir** is *to attend.*
>
> Your attendance at next week's meeting is very important. In fact, it's important for you to attend as many meetings as possible.

conduct   1. verb: to direct, control, lead

Note: pronounced "kun - DUCT," it is **conducir** in Spanish.

The chairperson conducted the meeting in a very serious manner.

2. noun: behavior; how you act

Note: pronounced "KAN - duct," it is **comportamiento** in Spanish.

Because of his good conduct, he was released early from prison.

> **NOTICE!**
>
> In English, the Spanish word **conducto** is *pipe, conduit,* or *duct.*
>
> Central air conditioning systems use ducts to move cold air around the house.

diversion   something that takes away your attention; that distracts you

He had trouble studying for the exam because there were so many diversions.

> **NOTICE!**
>
> In English, the Spanish word **diversión** is usually *amusement.*
>
> Going to the circus is a great amusement for children and adults alike.

to divert   to change direction

The clever soldiers diverted the enemy's attention and escaped.

Note: The verb **divertirse** has many translations in English: *to enjoy oneself; have a good time; have fun.*

We always enjoy ourselves at the movies.

They had a good time at the beach today.

The little girl has fun playing with her new dolls.

lecture a speech (usually about an academic subject) given to a large group of students

The professor's lecture on ancient Greek art was very interesting.

 NOTICE!

In English, the Spanish word **lectura** is *reading.*

Every week we have a new reading assignment. The reading for next week is a group of poems by Alfred Lord Tennyson.

to lecture to give a speech

The professor lectured about Latin American politics yesterday.

Note: to lecture somebody means **sermonear a alguien**

The parents lectured their children on the dangers of accepting rides from strangers.

Mass / mass the Catholic religious service, celebration of the Eucharist

Every Sunday morning, we go to church to hear Mass.

NOTICE!

In English, the Spanish word **masa** can be *dough.*

My mother gets up early in the morning and makes the dough so we can have fresh, homemade bread.

prosecution a legal action against somebody, usually the government's attorney (the district attorney) who is against a defendant

If Lee Harvey Oswald hadn't been killed, the prosecution against him would have been covered by the media all over the world.

NOTICE!

In English, the Spanish word **prosecución** can be *continuation.*

The continuation of his studies depended on his having a scholarship.

to prosecute   to bring a criminal charge against somebody

> The district attorney prosecuted the woman for stealing thousands of dollars from her employer.

rendition   an interpretation of a musical or dramatic work

> That actress' rendition of the role of Ophelia in *Hamlet* is the best I've ever seen.

NOTICE!

In English, the Spanish word **rendición** is *surrender* or *submission*.

> The surrender of the British General Cornwallis ended the American Revolution.

> The people's submission to the authority of the king was complete.

to render   1. to submit, give

> The carpenter rendered a bill for more money than we had expected.

2. to offer

> I'd be happy to render you some assistance if you need it.

reunion   a sentimental, emotional meeting between people who haven't seen each other for a long time

> Once every five years, we have a family reunion so that we can see all of our relatives.

NOTICE!

In English, the Spanish word **reunión** is *meeting* and it does not have any of the emotional meaning of the English word *reunion*.

> We'll have our next business meeting on the first Tuesday in May.

smoking the act of inhaling and exhaling cigarette smoke, or using cigars or pipes

Smoking is not permitted in almost all public buildings in the United States.

 NOTICE!

In English, the Spanish word **smoking (esmoquin)** is *tuxedo*.

He wore a dark blue tuxedo at his sister's wedding.

It's Under Construction

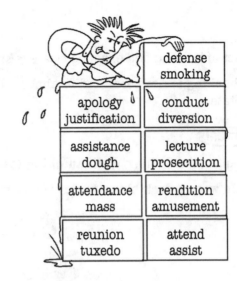

	defense smoking
apology justification	conduct diversion
assistance dough	lecture prosecution
attendance mass	rendition amusement
reunion tuxedo	attend assist

Choose any two-word block. Write a sentence using both words. Write in pencil or erasable ink. Then choose another block and write another sentence. Keep going until you've used up all nine blocks.

1. _____

2. _____

3. _____

4. _____

5. _____

6. _____

7. _____

8. _____

9. _____

If you are in a class, exchange books with a partner. Read his/her sentences and let him/her read yours. If either of you finds any errors, discuss them and make any necessary corrections.

As I Was Saying . . .

Complete the following mini-conversations by using the list of vocabulary words for this unit. Each conversation has two speakers, Person A and Person B.

amusement   assistance   conduct   meeting   smoking
apology   attendance   diversion   reunion   surrendered
mass

1. A: Does your church have good _____ on Sundays?

    B: Yes, many people come. It's because the priest who says _____ gives very interesting sermons.

2. A: What's this hotel reservation I found on top of the dresser?

    B: I think you've been working much too hard lately. You need a _____, so we're going to Key West for a long weekend. Surprise!

3. A: Young man, here's three dollars for helping me so much. I really appreciated your _____ with all those grocery bags.

    B: You're very welcome. And thank you.

4. A: What do you like to do for _____ ?

    B: Watch my dog and cat play together. It's really cute.

5. A: Now that the wedding is over, I owe you and your family a/an _____.

    B: We think so, too, Father.

    A: I'm so sorry that I called your son the wrong name during the ceremony.

6. A: How do people protect their houses from lightning?

    B: With lightning rods. They're metal rods that _____ the electricity from the lightning into the ground instead of the house.

7. A: What did the doctor recently tell you to stop doing?

    B: She told me to stop _____ . It's a very bad habit.

8. A: Are you going to your family _____ next month?

    B: Yes, actually. I'm looking forward to seeing everybody. Say, look at the time. We're almost late for our 3 o'clock _____ with the accountant. Let's go.

9. A: Did the police finally catch those hijackers?

    B: Yes. After a whole day of holding the truck driver hostage, the hijackers finally _____ to the police. I'm happy to say that the truck driver is fine.

ALTA BOOK
CENTER
PUBLISHERS ID

14 Adrian Court
Burlingame
California, 94010
USA

Luis Quintero

Let's I.D. Them!

Work alone or with a partner. The exercise is on this and the next page. If you work with a partner, one of you has this page and the other one will work with the next page. Choose your page. Now get started.

Here's what to do if you work with a partner. If not, just write in your answers on both pages.

- Read No. 1 to your partner and write down his/her I.D. on the line provided.

- Then your partner will read No. 2 to you. You make the I.D. and he/she will write it down just as you did.

- Now you read No. 3 and keep working this way until you're all done. Wait for your teacher to review the correct answers and then score your partner's answers.

Each answer = 10 points.

Exercise 1-A   I.D.

1. This is something that's fun to do, like dressing in costumes
    and masks on Halloween.   _____

3. The leaders of orchestras do this.   _____

5. This is what they have in Catholic churches every Sunday.   _____

7. This is an emotional get-together after a long time has passed.   _____

9. This is what you get when you mix flour and water.   _____

Exercise 2-A   I.D.

1. This is what you offer somebody when you're sorry.   _____

3. Keep doing this and you could get lung cancer.   _____

5. This is something you do to take attention away from
    something or somebody.   _____

7. This is another word for *help.*   _____

9. When people get together for business, they schedule one   _____
    of these.

Score: _____ points

Read the instructions on the previous page and you'll know what to do. Remember, when you score your partner's answers or your own, each one = 10 points.

Exercise 1-B   **I.D.**

2. This is the action of being present.   _____

4. This is when you explain the reasons for doing something.   _____

6. Water moves through these into our houses.   _____

8. This is somebody's interpretation of a song, poem, or speech.   _____

10. This is what soldiers do when they realize
    the other side has won a battle.   _____

Exercise 2-B   **I.D.**

2. On Christmas Eve, people like to go to this at midnight.   _____

4. My high school friends have one of these every five years.   _____

6. Men can wear this to very formal affairs, like weddings.   _____

8. Walt Disney World is the greatest example of this kind of park.   _____

10. Many cities have emergency phone numbers if you need this.   _____

Score: _____ **points**

Face to Face

Part A

Work alone or with a partner. Use this and the next page. If you work with somebody, decide who will look only at this page and who will look only at the next one.

By yourself: Read number 1 and then choose the best response from the next page. Continue through number 5, then start with number 6 on the next page and choose the response from this page.

With a partner: Read number 1 to your partner and he/she will select the best response from the other page. Continue until number 6. Now reverse how you do the exercise.

1. Don't you think we could use a diversion from nothing but work, work, work?

2. I hear the plumber is coming over today.

3. Should I play the part of Julius Caesar more passively or aggressively?

4. What was the greatest amusement for the ancient Romans?

5. What are you going to wear at your sister's wedding?

_____

6. a) Okay, I'll schedule a reunion right away.

   b) Okay, I'll schedule a meeting right away.

   c) Okay, I'll schedule a strategy right away.

7. a) Not until you give me an apology.

   b) Not until you lament what you did.

   c) Not until you say you feel it.

8. a) I know. He's almost never absent.

   b) I know. He's quite popular.

   c) I know. He helps her all the time.

9. a) It's going to be an incredible reunion!

   b) It's going to be an incredible amusement!

   c) It's going to be an incredible meeting!

10. a) Because of his poor assistance.

    b) Because of his poor attendance.

    c) Because of his poor present.

Face to Face

Part B

1. a) Okay, let's call your mother.

   b) Okay, let's take a vacation.

   c) Okay, we'll do some more.

2. a) Yes, he is. He has to replace some pipes in the bathroom.

   b) Yes, he is. He has to replace some conducts in the bathroom.

   c) Yes, he is. He has to replace some tubes in the bathroom.

3. a) Which temper do you think will work best?

   b) Which action do you think will work best?

   c) Which rendition do you think will work best?

4. a) I think it was pork.

   b) I think it was classical music.

   c) I think it was gladiatorial fights in the arena.

5. a) A new smoking I just bought.

   b) A new tuxedo I just bought.

   c) A new robe I just bought.

6. We have to sit down together with them and talk about our strategy.

7. Aren't you ever going to talk to me again?

8. The teacher appreciates his assistance in biology class.

9. Can you imagine? They haven't seen each other in twenty-five years!

10. Why does the school counselor want to see him?

Unit 8: Stative Verbs

My Word!

agonize   to struggle or fight with your own feelings

She agonized about whether or not to fire her secretary.

 NOTICE!

In English, the Spanish word **agonizar** means *to be dying*.

A hospice is a special kind of hospital where highly trained people tend to those who are dying.

agony   great pain

Until the medication started working, she was in agony.

notice   to observe; be aware of

I've noticed that Irving is very nervous today. Do you know what's bothering him?

 NOTICE!

In English, the Spanish word **noticia(s)** means *news*.

Note: Even though "news" looks like a plural word, it's singular in English.

The international news is very interesting today.

notice   a public/formal announcement in writing

There's a notice on the wall in the employees' lounge that smoking in this building is prohibited.

 NOTICE!

The Spanish word for *notice* in this case is **aviso** and *to notify* is **avisar.**

The management notified the employees that they couldn't smoke in the building anymore.

realize to comprehend completely or correctly

> After looking for a job for a few weeks, I realized it wasn't going to be as easy as I had thought it would be.

realization the act of realizing

> The realization that it wouldn't be easy to find a job made me worried.

The Spanish word for this idea of *realize* is the phrase **darse cuenta**.

recollect to remember

> I recollect that we met back in 1992. Am I right?

In English, the Spanish word **recolectar** means *to gather* or *to gather in.*

> Every evening, the farmer gathers in his sheep for the night.

recollection the act of remembering

> Most people have no recollection of their first two or three years of life.

Going  Blank

Here is a list of the words you have just learned. Use them in the blanks that follow. Don't use a word more than once. Enjoy.

is agonizing	*gather*	*notice*	*realized*
am dying	*news*	*notify*	*recollect*

1. A: There's an interesting _____ in today's paper.

   B: Really? What's it for?

   A: Mt. Sinai Hospital is looking for volunteers to try out a new vaccine they're experimenting with. They'll pay volunteers a lot of money, they say.

2. A: Ooh. My poor stomach. I feel like I _____.

   B: What's the matter?

   A: I drank a whole glass of milk before I _____ that it didn't smell too good.

   B: Oh. So you drank milk that had turned bad. Now I know why you're sick.

3. A: Janice has a lot on her mind right now.

   B: Why?

   A: Haven't you heard the _____ ? She's been offered a great career opportunity with our competition.

   B: I haven't heard anything about it. So, is she going to accept the new job?

   A: She can't make up her mind whether to stay here where she feels loyalty or go over to the competition. She _____ over what to do.

   B: Well, it's great that she's in demand!

   A: Well, if my memory serves me right, I _____ that you haven't had job offers like that.

B: True, but that's because everyone knows I'd never leave our company.

A: Even if you were offered double your current salary?

4. A: You know, my favorite American holiday is Thanksgiving.

B: Why is that?

A: Because the members of each family _____ together to enjoy being with one another. It's a wonderful time for families.

B: Yes, I guess it is.

A: It's always fun to recall our childhood moments.

5. A: How do passengers know which gates their planes leave from?

B: The airlines _____ them by putting the information on TV screens at various places in the airport.

ALTA BOOK
CENTER
PUBLISHERS ID

14 Adrian Court
Burlingame
California, 94010
USA

Luis Quintero

Let's I.D. Them!

Work alone or with a partner. The exercise is on this and the next page. If you work with a partner, one of you has this page and the other one will work with the next page. Choose your page. Now get started.

Here's what to do if you work with a partner. If not, just write in your answers on both pages.

• Read No. 1 to your partner and write down his/her I.D. on the line provided.

• Then your partner will read No. 2 to you. You make the I.D. and he/she will write it down just as you did.

• Now read No. 3 and keep working this way until you're all done. Wait for your teacher to review the correct answers and then score your partner's answers.

Each answer = 10 points.

Exercise A   **I.D.**

1. This is what you watch on TV or read in the paper.   _____

3. It means to suffer mental pain of some kind.   _____

5. This means to let people know some information.   _____

7. When people are in a hospice, they're doing this.   _____

9. This means to observe something.   _____

Score: _____ **points**

Read the instructions on the previous page and you'll know what to do. Remember, when you score your partner's answers or your own, each one = 10 points.

Exercise B   I.D.

2. This is another word for *remember*.   _____

4. When you bring things or people together, you do this.   _____

6. This means to figure out or understand.   _____

8. In English, people often say "Aha!" when they do this.   _____

10. The word that means *great pain* comes from this verb. _____

Score: _____ **points**

This  or  That?

Circle the right word for each of these sentences.

1. Was it that radio show that **noticed / notified** him he'd won a trip to Paris?

2. I'm so happy. Most of today's **news / notice** is good for a change.

3. A: Have you heard about poor Sammy?

   B: No. What's going on?

   A: He's **dying / agonizing** in the hospital.

   B: No! I'm so sorry to hear that. Is there anything we can do?

4. A: Remember when we were kids and your father would **recollect / gather** all the neighborhood kids and have a barbecue?

   B: Yep. I **recollect / gather** that very well. Those were good times.

The Cognate Repair Shop

Correct any vocabulary errors you find in the following sentences. Work on your own or with a partner.

1. A: Albert looks like he's agonizing. What's the matter with him?

    B: He's been exercising in the gym too much and he's not used to that.

2. A: Let's turn on the TV and watch the notices on Channel 10.

    B: Okay. I want to find out the election results.

3. A: Do you know what I did with the remote control?

    B: No, I don't. Can't you gather where you left it?

4. A: Jimmy! Please recollect all your toys and put them in the box I gave you for that purpose.

    B: Okay, Mom.

SECTION 2
Words We Use Sometimes

Unit 1: People and Other Living Things

My Word!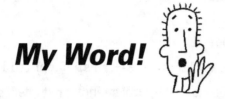

animator   a professional artist who makes movies from drawings

She worked as an animator for the Disney Studios for many years.

 NOTICE!

In English, **animador** is *master of ceremonies.* The person is also called the *emcee* (m.c. = master of ceremonies).

Billy Crystal was the master of ceremonies for the Academy Awards show.

to animate   to make movies with drawings

She specialized in animating certain Disney characters like "Pluto."

 NOTICE!

In English, the Spanish word **animar** is *to enliven* or *to encourage.*

He needed caffeine to enliven his senses.

She encouraged her husband to stay on his diet.

auditor   a professional who conducts financial or fiscal investigations

To keep the business "honest," two auditors look at the company's books every year.

 NOTICE!

In English, the Spanish word **auditor** is *judge advocate.*

The judge advocate will hear your lawsuit.

to audit   1. to investigate a company's books and finances

While auditing the company's books, he found two discrepancies.

2. to take a college course without getting credit for it

> I was taking so many courses for a grade that I decided simply to audit the biology course.

brute

1. a big animal or beast

> I can't believe how large your German shepherd is. He's a brute!

2. a person who depends on physical strength, not intellect, to accomplish things

> That brute only knows one way to settle arguments—with his fists.

 NOTICE!

In English, the Spanish word **bruto** can be *stupid* or *dumb.*

> He acted dumb when the police questioned him about the robbery.

dame

woman (not considered very polite by some speakers)

> I see the boss hired a new dame to be his secretary.

 NOTICE!

In English, the Spanish **dama** is *lady.*

> She works in a clothing store exclusively for ladies.

Dame

a title of honor and respect for a woman in Great Britain given only by the monarch for something special the woman has done

> Dame Judith Anderson was a well-respected British actress.

hippo

a short word for hippopotamus

> The hippo was in the river, peacefully eating aquatic plants.

NOTICE!

In English, the Spanish word **hipo** is *hiccup / hiccough* (different spelling, same pronunciation).

She gets hiccups when she drinks milk too fast.

lime   a small citrus fruit, which is always green when ripe

In many Latin American countries, it's popular to cook meat, poultry, and fish with lime juice.

 NOTICE!

Remember that *limes* are always *green* when ripe. The small citrus fruit that is *yellow* when ripe is called a *lemon.*

My mother always puts lemon in her tea.

recipient   a person who has received something

It's always nice to be the recipient of good news.

 NOTICE!

In English, the Spanish word **recipiente** is *container.*

We keep coffee in a plastic container in the refrigerator.

recluse   somebody who likes to stay alone

He just stays by himself all the time in his little house in the woods. He's become a real recluse.

NOTICE!

In English, the Spanish word **recluso** is *prisoner* or *inmate.*

In our state prisons, there are usually four inmates to a cell.

syndicate   1. an association of people formed for business reasons or to sell and distribute articles or columns for newspapers and magazines

My friend works for a large syndicate that handles newspaper comic strips like "Popeye" and "Little Orphan Annie."

2. an organized crime group like the Mafia

When casinos opened in Atlantic City, New Jersey, the police commissioner was worried that the syndicate would try to take control and establish organized crime.

NOTICE!

In English, the Spanish word **sindicato** is *labor union* or simply *union.*

Labor unions protect the rights of workers and help improve their working conditions and salaries.

in syndication   when a newspaper column or television show is distributed by a company to newspapers, television stations, and so on to be shown in many places at the same time

Episodes of the old television show *I Love Lucy* are now shown in syndication all over the United States and in other countries, too.

syndicated   shown in many newspapers, many television channels, or many radio stations at the same time

He's a syndicated columnist whose newspaper articles are very popular.

tramp   1. an unemployed person who has no home and keeps moving from town to town

Tramps used to travel around the country for free by hiding in the cars of freight trains.

2. a woman with no morals about sex

Nobody will want to marry her. She's been a tramp all her life.

 NOTICE!

In English, the Spanish word **trampa** is *trick* or *trap.*

Don't believe what that salesman is telling you. It's just a trap to make you buy more.

vigilante   a person who takes the law into his own hands and persecutes somebody accused of a crime before the person is proven to be guilty in a court of law

Many innocent people have died at the hands of vigilantes who hanged them before they could have fair trials.

NOTICE!

In English, the Spanish word **vigilante** is *guard* or *watchman.*

He works as a guard in the emergency room of this hospital.

vigilant   watchful; on the alert

The vigilant soldiers made sure the enemy didn't pass their lines.

Going  Blank

Here's a list of the words you have just learned. Use them in the blanks that follow. You may not be able to use all of them in these passages. Don't use a word more than one time. Enjoy.

animator	brute	dame	recluse	tramp
auditor	Dame	hippos	syndicate	vigilantes
		recipient		

Selection No. 1

In the 1920s, a young film _____ named Walt Disney decided to move to

Hollywood, California to start a studio of his own. He had invented many animal characters

for his short films, like giraffes, elephants, and _____ , but the character that got

his attention the most was a mouse, which he named "Mickey." Today Mickey Mouse is

known all over the world and Walt Disney Studios is the _____ of many awards for

the cartoons that Mickey Mouse has starred in.

Selection No. 2

This is a conversation between Allan and Bob, two factory workers.

Allan: Hey, Bob, how's it going?

Bob: Not bad. Have you seen the new _____ the boss just hired to check the

company's books? She's a real pretty _____ .

Allan: Oh? Are you interested in her?

Bob: Yeah, but she won't get friendly with anyone. She acts like a real _____ and just

stays in her office all day.

Allan: Too bad. But just remember, Bob, there are many good fish in the sea!

Selection No. 3

Pistol Pete had a wild and strange career in crime in the Old West. At the age of fifteen he ran away from home and lived like a _____ for a few years, moving from place to place by secretly riding in the stock cars of trains. Pete was a real _____ who thought the best way to solve any problem with another person was by beating up that person.

Then one day, when Pete was in Dodge City, he met "_____ Betty," a woman who worked in the largest bar in town. The locals had given her that British title because she was born in London and thought she was better than everybody else. It turned out that Betty worked for the local crime_____ who dealt with prostitution and bank robbing. Pete and Betty became a hot item together and were doing well in their life of crime. They weren't very careful, however, and the local group of _____ caught them trying to rob a bank all by themselves. That was the end. They were taken to the nearest tall tree and. . . well, you can imagine the rest.

ALTA BOOK
CENTER
PUBLISHERS ID

14 Adrian Court
Burlingame
California, 94010
USA

Luis Quintero

Let's I.D. Them!

Work alone or with a partner. The exercise is on this and the next page. If you work with a partner, one of you has this page and the other one will work with the next page. Choose your page. Now get started.

Here's what to do if you work with a partner. If not, just write in your answers on both pages.

- Read No. 1 to your partner and write down his/her I.D. on the line provided.
- Then your partner will read No. 2 to you. You make the I.D. and he/she will write it down just as you did.
- Now read No. 3 and keep working this way until you're all done. Wait for your teacher to review the correct answers and then score your partner's answers.

Each answer = 10 points.

Exercise 1-A   I.D.

1. This is the person in charge of a game or talk show on TV.   _____

3. This type of person is unemployed and moves from town   _____
   to town.

5. These are people who are kept in jail or prison.   _____

7. You can put things in this.   _____

9. This animal lives in African rivers.   _____

Exercise 2-A   I.D.

1. When you get these, you make a funny sound and feel like   _____
   your stomach is trying to jump into your throat.

3. The Queen of England gave her this title.   _____

5. This is the person who will control the court during a trial.   _____

7. This is a person who gets something.   _____

9. This person draws movie cartoons for a living.   _____

Score: _____ points

Read the instructions on the previous page and you'll know what to do. Remember, when you score your partner's answers or your own, each one = 10 points.

Exercise 1-B   **I.D.**

2. This means *watchful* or *alert*.   _____

4. This is another word for *woman*.   _____

6. This is another word for *the mafia*.   _____

8. They don't want to wait for justice to punish a criminal.   _____

10. This citrus fruit should be green before you use it.   _____

Exercise 2-B   **I.D.**

2. You call this person to check financial records.   _____

4. This person doesn't use his brain to win an argument,
   only his strength.   _____

6. This person wants to be alone.   _____

8. This company distributes newspaper columns
   around the country.   _____

10. This woman has had many, many sexual affairs.   _____

Score: _____ **points**

This 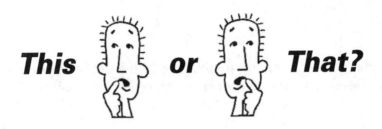 or That?

Circle the right word for each of these sentences.

1. Ralph loves to play **tramps / tricks** on his friends.

2. Please take the flour out of the bag and put it into that **container / recipient**.

3. You need a lot of talent to be a good **emcee / animator** in a nightclub.

4. He got a good night job as a **guard / vigilante** in a local factory.

5. She wore a **lime / lemon** yellow dress and a **lime / lemon** green jacket.

6. Of all the **inmates / recluses** in this jail, Johnson and Smith are such **inmates / recluses**; they never want to socialize with the others.

7. Auto workers have one of the strongest **syndicates / unions** in the U.S.

8. King World is a/an **syndicate / union** that distributes old television shows to TV stations all around the U.S.

9. You need to have a lot of talent to be a good **emcee / animator** for *Looney Tunes* and other cartoon films.

10. Many black men were unjustly hanged by **guards / vigilantes** in the American South back in the early part of the 20th century.

The Cognate Repair Shop

Correct any vocabulary errors you find in the following sentences. Work on your own or with a partner.

1. Johnny Carson is a famous American animator who had a television talk show called *The Tonight Show*.

2. This clothing store is for men and that one is for dames.

3. Please get me some water. I've got hippo.

4. Oh, no! We have no recipient to put this sugar in.

5. Our warehouse is very safe. We've hired five more vigilantes to protect it.

6. Trying to lift that big, heavy rock by yourself is a brute thing to do. You'll end up hurting your back.

7. Some recluses will be moved to another prison because there are too many here.

8. I'd like to make some ceviche. Do we have any more lemons?

9. This case has had a lot of publicity. I hope we get the right auditor to hear all the evidence when the trial begins.

10. If you want to work and have a good job in this town, you should become a member of the syndicate.

Unit 2: Concrete Things

My Word!

balsa   a tropical tree with very light, buoyant wood

People like to use balsa wood to carve things because it's so easy to cut.

 NOTICE!

In English, the Spanish word **balsa** is *raft*.

Rafts are mostly used for transportation in slow-moving water.

barb   a short, sharp, pointed object that can enter your skin and hurt a lot

Some plants and animals have barbs on their bodies for protection.

 NOTICE!

Don't confuse the English word *barb* with the Spanish word **barba**. In English, **barba** is *beard*.

In Ancient Greece, it was customary for adult men not to shave their faces. Their beards were a sign of maturity.

cadaver   a dead human body used for medical education or research

> When medical students learn about anatomy, they must dissect cadavers obtained from the county morgue.

 NOTICE!

In normal, conversational English, the Spanish word **cadáver** is *dead body* or *corpse.*

> The police found a dead body lying on the side of the road.

cargo   transported merchandise carried by a ship, plane, or other vehicle

> Airlines make a lot of money by carrying cargo in addition to passengers.

NOTICE!

1. In English, the Spanish word **cargo** is *duty* or *responsibility*. Also, the phrase **estar a cargo de** is *to be in charge of* in English.

> An airplane pilot is in charge of the safety of all the passengers and the crew.

2. job, position

> He's held many (elected) positions in government.

confection   a sweet preparation like candy or marmalade

> I have a "sweet tooth." I love to eat all kinds of confections.

NOTICE!

Don't confuse the English word *confection* with the Spanish word **confección**. In English, **confección** is *manufactured goods, tailoring,* or *the making of something.*

That factory produces all kinds of manufactured goods.

All of his suits have custom tailoring (are custom tailored). That's why they're so expensive.

The making of computers is still a developing field.

curriculum   all the courses offered at a school

The curriculum at my son's high school is very diverse, although it focuses on technological courses.

NOTICE!

Currículo can have the English meaning, but it also can mean a history of a person's work experience. In that case, **currículo** is a *résumé* in English.

Every time I apply for a job, I send the company a letter with a copy of my résumé.

Note: "Résumé" is pronounced "reh-zoo-MAY." Don't confuse it with another English word, *resume,* pronounced "ree-ZOOM." *Resume* means to start something again after you have stopped or paused for awhile.

We've been working on these contracts for almost three hours. Let's stop for lunch. Then we'll resume the meeting.

dormitory   a building on a university campus where students live in individual or shared rooms

There used to be separate dormitories for men and women at this university, but things have changed.

 NOTICE!

In English, the Spanish word **dormitorio** is *bedroom.*

I have my computer on a desk in my bedroom.

gala   a large and very formal party or ball

There was a gala in Hollywood to celebrate the opening of the movie *Titanic*. All the big stars were there.

In English, the Spanish word **gala** is *fine clothes*.

The Hollywood celebrities were in their finest clothes for the opening of *Titanic*.

idiom   an expression whose words do not literally mean what they say

"It's raining cats and dogs" is an idiom in the English language. It means that it's raining very hard.

NOTICE!

In English, the Spanish word **idioma** is *language*.

Did you know that Marvin can speak six languages?

marmalade   a thick, sweet confection made from oranges or other citrus fruit that is spread on bread or toast

In many countries, it's common to spread orange marmalade on toast for breakfast.

NOTICE!

The Spanish word **mermelada** is a confection made from many kinds of fruit. In English, *marmalade* is made only from citrus fruit.

Moreover, the Spanish word **conserva** can be *jelly* or *jam/preserves* in English. You say *jelly* if it's clear, but *jam* or *preserves* if there are pieces of fruit in it.

> I know you like marmalade on your toast, but have you ever tried apple jelly? It's delicious!

> There are a lot of varieties of jelly and jam in the supermarket, but my favorite has always been strawberry jam/preserves.

pastel   delicate, light color

> On Caribbean islands, you usually see houses painted in beautiful pastel colors, especially pink, blue, and peach.

Don't confuse the English *pastel* with the Spanish word **pastel,** which is *pastry, pie,* or *cake* in English.

> This is the most delicious pastry I've ever eaten!

pentagram   a star with five points; a sign of the devil or other evil creatures

> In East European folklore, the pentagram is the sign of the werewolf.

Don't confuse the English *pentagram* with the Spanish word **pentagrama,** which is a *musical staff* in English.

The fancy ♪ at the beginning of sheet music is the staff sign.

pimiento a sweet red bell pepper, usually roasted and used in dishes to give a special flavor and color (also written *pimento,* which is the way it is pronounced: "pih-MEN-toh")

> Many Americans like to eat a certain kind of cold luncheon meat called olive and pimiento loaf. It is a kind of bologna with pieces of olive and pimiento in it.

NOTICE!

In English, the Spanish word **pimienta** is *(black) pepper.*

> Please pass me the salt and pepper.

pinto a horse with irregular marks on its body

> The pinto mare had big brown spots.

NOTICE!

In English, the Spanish word **pinto** is *spotted* or *speckled.*

> In English we call that horse a "pinto" because of the Spanish influence. The horse's coloring is spotted.

refrain the part of a poem or song that is repeated a few times

> She only knows the refrains of many songs.

NOTICE!

In English, the Spanish word **refrán** is a *proverb* or *saying.*

> What's that old saying? Oh yes, "Money doesn't grow on trees."

to refrain   to decide or agree not to do something

> In many public buildings, you must refrain from smoking.

resort   a place where people go for relaxation and recreation

> Miami Beach and Cancún are famous for their luxurious resorts where people can stay for a few days or even weeks and enjoy all the facilities.

In English, the Spanish word **resorte** is *spring.*

> The springs in my mattress are old. I almost sink to the floor when I lie down on my bed!

talon   the sharp claw or nail of a bird of prey like an eagle or hawk

> The eagle flew down and grabbed the rabbit with its giant talons.

> **NOTICE!**

In English, the Spanish word **talón** is *heel* (of the foot).

These shoes are too tight around my heels. They really hurt.

vapor   1. usually water that has evaporated into the air

The humidity here is produced by the vapor from the swamps.

2. in the plural, fumes that are given off by such things as menthol, turpentine, ammonia, etc.

You should always keep your windows open when you're working with turpentine. If you don't, you can breathe in too much of the vapors that it produces and get sick.

> **NOTICE!**

In English, vapor is not necessarily hot. The thing that is hot is *steam.*

The first powerful engines in the 19th century were steam engines.

It's Under Construction

idiom	vapor

cadaver resort	pinto pastel

barbs talons	balsa pentagram

dormitory confection	refrain curriculum

gala pimiento	raft beards

Choose any two-word block. Write a sentence using both words. Write in pencil or erasable ink. Then choose another block and write another sentence. Keep going until you've used up all nine blocks.

1. _____

2. _____

3. _____

4. _____

5. _____

6. _____

7. _____

8. _____

9. _____

If you are in a class, exchange books with a partner. Read his/her sentences and let him/her read yours. If either of you finds any errors, discuss them and make any necessary corrections.

As I Was Saying . . .

Complete the following mini-conversations by using the list of vocabulary words for this unit.
Each conversation has two speakers, Person A and Person B.

cadavers	*dead body*	*gala*	*pastel*	*talons*
curriculum	*dormitories*	*idiom*	*resort*	*vapor*

1. A: I'm so excited about the city celebrating its centennial, aren't you?

    B: Of course I am. And I can't wait to go to the _____ at City Hall. It'll be the best and biggest party you've ever seen!

2. A: It's getting really late. Would you like to sleep over?

    B: What does *sleep over* mean? I don't understand.

    A: It's a/an _____ . It means spend the night here.

3. A: What colors is Miami famous for?

    B: That's easy. Aquamarine and pink, especially the _____ shades.

4. A: Did you listen to the news on TV last night?

    B: No, I was busy. What did they report?

    A: That a/an _____ was found floating in a canal behind the apartment building at 750 Northwest 20th Street.

    B: 750 Northwest 20th Street? Oh, no! That's where my cousin Irene lives!

4. A: Gosh! Have you seen the fancy, new _____ that the college has built for the students?

    B: No, I haven't.

    A: Well, you just won't believe your eyes. They're so beautiful and have so many facilities that they're more like a/an _____ than anything else!

5. A: Where does the medical school get the _____ that are used for anatomy classes?

    B: From the county morgue. They're bodies that nobody has claimed.

6. A: I like the new _____ the college has decided to follow.

    B: Yeah, it has a lot more art courses in it.

7. A: Why do owls and eagles have such sharp _____ ?

    B: So that they can catch their prey easily.

8. A: What's dew?

    B: Dew? Why, that's drops of water you find on plants in the early morning. Dew forms when water _____ condenses on the leaves.

ALTA BOOK
CENTER
PUBLISHERS ID

14 Adrian Court
Burlingame
California, 94010
USA

Luis Quintero

Let's I.D. Them!

Work alone or with a partner. The exercise is on this and the next page. If you work with a partner, one of you has this page and the other one will work with the next page. Choose your page. Now get started.

Here's what to do if you work with a partner. If not, just write in your answers on both pages.

- Read No. 1 to your partner and write down his/her I.D. on the line provided.

- Then your partner will read No. 2 to you. You make the I.D. and he/she will write it down just as you did.

- Now read No. 3 and keep working this way until you're all done. Wait for your teacher to review the correct answers and then score your partner's answers.

Each answer = 10 points.

Exercise A   **I.D.**

1. It's where college students can live on campus.   _____

3. This is what doctors call a dead body.   _____

5. This horse has colors "splashed" across it.   _____

7. People use this sweet red pepper to cook with.   _____

9. "He turned green with envy" is one of these.   _____

11. Some fish have these sharp points which can easily
    penetrate skin.   _____

13. Birds such as eagles have these on their feet.   _____

15. This is a hotel with a sauna, nightclub, golf course, and casino. _____

17. This wood is very light and easy to carve.   _____

19. This is a star with five points.   _____

Score: _____ **points**

Read the instructions on the previous page and you'll know what to do. Remember, when you score your partner's answers or your own, each one = 10 points.

Exercise B   **I.D.**

2. This is all the courses offered at a school.   _____

4. This is merchandise carried on a plane or ship.   _____

6. This is a very formal, big event to celebrate something.   _____

8. Vapor isn't always hot, but this is.   _____

10. This is a soft, delicate color.   _____

12. This is another word people use for a dead body.   _____

14. You can see this in the form of mist rising over a lake
in the early morning when the temperature is cool.   _____

16. This is sweet and made from oranges or other citrus fruit. _____

18. This is sweet and made with pieces of fruit in it.   _____

20. This is sweet and made from fruit, but without pieces
of fruit in it.   _____

Score: _____ **points**

 **Face to Face**

Part A

Work alone or with a partner. Use this and the next page. If you work with somebody, decide who will look only at this page and who will look only at the next one.

By yourself: Read number 1 and then choose the best response from the next page. Continue through number 5, then start with number 6 on the next page and choose the response from this page.

With a partner: Read number 1 to your partner and he/she will select the best response from the other page. Continue until number 6. Now reverse how you do the exercise.

1. How did they travel from one island to the other?

2. I'm going to the supermarket.

3. Why is that room always so cold?

4. Helen has a brand new car. I'm green with envy.

5. I'm going to apply for that job on Monday.

---

6. a) Okay, I'll use the extra bed in your alcove.

   b) Okay, I'll use the extra bed in your bedroom.

   c) Okay, I'll use the extra bed in your dormitory.

7. a) I'll get some confection at the bakery.

   b) I'll get some pastel at the bakery.

   c) I'll get some pastry at the bakery.

8. a) I like that saying.

   b) I like that idiom.

   c) I like that refrain.

9. a) I hear it's a wonderful country.

   b) I hear it's a wonderful resort.

   c) I hear it's a wonderful beach.

10. a) With this cold I can't breathe through my nose. Breathing in the vapors will help.

    b) With this cold I can't breathe through my nose. Breathing in the airs will help.

    c) With this cold I can't breathe through my nose. Breathing in the steam will help.

Face to Face

Part B

1. a) On balsas.

   b) On tree trunks.

   c) On rafts.

2. a) Good. Please pick up some grape marmalade.

   b) Good. Please pick up some grape jelly.

   c) Good. Please pick up some grape confection.

3. a) It's where the medical school keeps the cadavers.

   b) It's where the medical school keeps the corpses.

   c) It's where the medical school keeps the dead bodies.

4. a) Green with envy? That's an interesting idiom.

   b) Green with envy? That's an interesting color.

   c) Green with envy? You should see a doctor about that.

5. a) Don't forget to take along your curriculum.

   b) Don't forget to take along your background.

   c) Don't forget to take along your résumé.

---

6. The weather is very bad. Why don't you sleep over at my house tonight?

7. We have everything we need for tonight's dinner except dessert.

8. "If at first you don't succeed, try, try again."

9. We're going to the Coral Village Hotel on our next vacation.

10. Why are you putting that mentholated cream all over your chest?

Unit 3: Words that Describe

My Word!

anticipated   expected

His anticipated arrival time was 9:00 PM.

NOTICE!

In English, the Spanish phrase **por anticipado** is *in advance*.

They took money out of the bank in advance when they were planning their trip to Europe.

to anticipate   to think about what's coming in the future; to expect

The National Hurricane Center anticipated that Hurricane Georges would not come on shore in Southeast Florida.

bland   1. not having much flavor or taste; unseasoned

People with stomach conditions like ulcers are told to eat bland foods.

2. unexciting; uninteresting (boring)

The colors of the paint used throughout the house were very bland: only white, beige, and light gray.

NOTICE!

In English, the Spanish word **blando** is *soft*.

That couch is so soft and comfortable that I always fall asleep if I lie on it.

candid   direct and frank; honest

> Do you really want me to give you a candid answer to that question? You may not like the truth.

NOTICE!

In English, the Spanish word **cándido** can be *simple* or *innocent.*

> There's really a very simple explanation as to why he did that.

> One reason adults like children so much is that they are so innocent; they don't know much about the world yet.

complacent   satisfied; content; accepting things too easily

> Sometimes, when people are complacent, they don't try to make anything better; they just live with it.

NOTICE!

In English, the Spanish word **complaciente** is *obliging* or *indulgent.*

> She's the most cooperative person I know. She's always so obliging whenever we need help.

> Grandparents are usually very indulgent when their grandchildren visit them; they let the grandchildren do anything.

complacence/   contentment; satisfaction
complacency
> Complacence is not always a good thing because then people never think about how they can do something in a better way.

crude   1. being vulgar

> She would never repeat the crude jokes her husband tells to his friends.

2. undeveloped; unrefined

> Crude oil is sent to a refinery, where it is processed and made into many products such as gasoline.

In English, the Spanish word **crudo** can be *raw.*

> You didn't cook this steak long enough. It's still raw inside!

eventual   occurring at an unspecified time in the future; something that will happen after enough time has passed

> As he was considered one of the best workers in the company, his eventual rise to a top position was expected by everyone.

eventually   finally; after enough time has passed

> Right now I like being a clerk in the store, but eventually I would like to be the manager.

In English, the Spanish word **eventual** is *incidental,* which means *of a minor or casual nature* or *not in the regular or important plan.*

> During his business trip to Bogotá, he had some incidental expenses which he didn't charge to his company.

> Much of the music you hear during a movie is called "incidental music."

fastidious   careful in all details

> The reason he's such a good secretary is that he's a fastidious worker. He never forgets any of the details and checks his work carefully.

In English, the Spanish word **fastidioso** is *annoying.*

> The constant buzz of the mosquitoes around her face was annoying.

In English, the Spanish word **fastidiar** is *to annoy,* which means *to bother* or *irritate.*

> Please stop tapping your fingers on the table. It really annoys me.

injected   forced into something (like a person's skin, arm, etc.)

> Years ago, insulin was a medicine that could only be injected; now there is an oral form of it, too.

In English, the Spanish word **inyectado** can be *bloodshot,* when the eyes look red inside.

> Because he had stayed up reading most of the night, his eyes were bloodshot in the morning.

to inject   to force one thing into another

> The doctor injected the vaccination into the boy's arm with a sterilized syringe.

injection   medicine given to a patient with a syringe

> Most people hate injections because they can be very painful.

insensible   unconscious

> When the door opened and hit him in the head, he became insensible and fell to the floor.

NOTICE!

In English, the Spanish word **insensible** usually means *insensitive, hard-hearted,* or *callous.*

> She was insensitive to other people's problems because she had gone through so many problems of her own.

plausible probable; apparently it could be or it could happen

> It's plausible that the United States will have a female president in the future.

 NOTICE!

In English, the Spanish word **plausible** is *praiseworthy.*

> His work is so praiseworthy that he's getting a large bonus and a promotion.

Going  Blank

Here's a list of the words you have just learned. Use them in the blanks that follow. You may not be able to use all of them in these passages. Don't use a word more than one time. Enjoy.

anticipated	candid	crude	fastidious	insensible
bland	complacent	eventual	injected	plausible

1. Frank, I'd like your _____ opinion about something. Be totally honest.

2. He liked his food _____, with almost no seasonings.

3. A: Your theory is ridiculous! In fact, most of your ideas are unbelievable!

   B: You may think they are, but I believe my theories are all very _____.

4. The election is only a month away and the _____ outcome is that the Democrats will win most of the offices unless people are too _____ and just sit at home instead of voting.

5. A: How did Jack ever survive the bite from that Indian cobra? He was _____ with enough venom to kill two men!

   B: I know! The poison was so powerful that he was _____ for a couple of days. It was like he was in a coma.

6. She's such a _____ house cleaner that you can eat off her floors!

7. Please don't tell me any more of those vulgar jokes. I don't appreciate your _____ sense of humor.

8. The Roman Empire was great and powerful, but its _____ fall was caused by a combination of economic and political pressures.

ALTA BOOK
CENTER
PUBLISHERS ID

14 Adrian Court
Burlingame
California, 94010
USA

Luis Quintero

Let's I.D. Them!

Work alone or with a partner. The exercise is on this and the next page. If you work with a partner, one of you has this page and the other one will work with the next page. Choose your page. Now get started.

Here's what to do if you work with a partner. If not, just write in your answers on both pages.

• Read No. 1 to your partner and write down his/her I.D. on the line provided.

• Then your partner will read No. 2 to you. You make the I.D. and he/she will write it down just as you did.

• Now read No. 3 and keep working this way until you're all done. Wait for your teacher to review the correct answers and then score your partner's answers.

Each answer = 10 points.

Exercise 1-A   I.D.

1. This means when you do something early or before you
    need it.   _____

3. This is when you just accept things too easily.   _____

5. This is something you've been waiting for.   _____

7. This is what you call somebody or something that bothers you. _____

9. It means *honest* or *frank*.   _____

Exercise 2-A   I.D.

1. Food with very little flavor or seasoning tastes this way. _____

3. Penicillin can be taken in the form of a pill, but it can also
    be given this way.   _____

5. You're this way if you pay attention to the smallest details. _____

7. Before oil is refined, it's in this condition.   _____

9. This word means after enough time has passed.   _____

Score: _____ points

Read the instructions on the previous page and you'll know what to do. Remember, when you score your partner's answers or your own, each one = 10 points.

Exercise 1-B   I.D.

2. If you're unconscious, you're like this.   _____

4. This means something is possible or believable.   _____

6. This means when you think something is going to happen.   _____

8. These are the kinds of expenses you might have on a
   business trip that don't relate directly to your business. _____

10. If you have no sympathy for others, you're this way.   _____

Exercise 2-B   I.D.

2. This is the condition when your eyes are all red.   _____

4. It can mean low class or uncultured.   _____

6. It's another way to say *finally.*   _____

8. Many people like pillows filled with feathers or down
   because that makes the pillows very _____.   _____

10. This means when you give someone whatever he/she wants.   _____

Score: _____ **points**

This 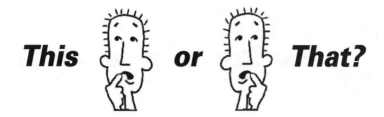 or 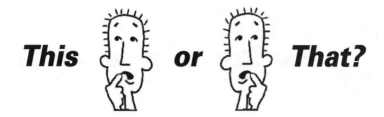 That?

Circle the right word for each of these sentences.

1. Some people think that flan is too **bland / soft** without the caramel topping.

2. When he hit his head on the side of the swimming pool, he became
    insensible / insensitive and had to be rescued by the lifeguard.

3. You always bring healthy food on our picnics. I see you have a platter full of
    raw / crude vegetables for us this time.

4. What she's done for that charity is very **plausible / praiseworthy**.

5. Don't you think her prediction was very **plausible / praiseworthy**?

6. I think not sending them a sympathy card when their father passed away was very
    insensible / callous.

7. You should stop sitting in front of a computer screen for so many hours each day. Just
    look at your eyes. They're all **bloodshot / injected**!

8. One reason we like him so much is that he's a **simple / candid** person who has
    no great desires.

9. The **future / anticipated** king of Fulania will be at a presidential reception given
    in his honor tonight.

10. Didn't you make these potatoes too **bland / soft**? They're falling apart.

The Cognate Repair Shop

Work on your own or with a partner. Correct any vocabulary errors you find in the following sentences.

1. Don't be so complacent to our neighbor just because you think she's so pretty.

2. I know the store is small, but incidentally we expect to grow much larger.

3. Her eyes always get injected after she's been up too late the night before.

4. I don't like a bland mattress. It always hurts my back if I sleep on one.

5. It's very fastidious when you arrive at the airport and find out that your flight has been delayed.

6. People in France eat a dish called steak tartare. It's crude ground beef with seasonings.

7. Did you have any eventual expenses on your last business trip?

8. She's a great soccer player, isn't she? Her performance on the playing field is always plausible.

9. Look! You made her cry. That was a very insensible remark you made.

10. This is only a raw model of the machine. Wait until we've had time to refine it.

Unit 4: Active Verbs

My Word!

contest   to dispute, challenge

> Because their dead uncle hadn't left them anything in his will, they contested the will to get some of his money.

 NOTICE!

In English, the Spanish word **contestar** is *to answer.*

> I asked you a question. Could you please answer me?

Note: The pronunciation of this verb is "kun - TEST." Don't confuse it with the noun, *contest,* pronounced "KAN - test," which is **concurso** in Spanish.

> For winning the national history contest, the school was awarded a multimedia center.

declassify   to remove official security classification (from a document)

> In recent years, the American government has declassified many of the documents dealing with the assassination of President John F. Kennedy so that the public can read them.

 NOTICE!

In English, the Spanish word **desclasificar** is *to disqualify.*

> They disqualified him from the contest for cheating.

declassification the act of declassifying

> The declassification of documents about the assassination of JFK has created a great deal of renewed interest in the case among the public.

esteem respect (usually with the adjectives *high* [meaning *much*] or *low* [meaning *little*])

> Ms. Cadbury is held in high esteem by all the employees.

to esteem to respect; place a high value on something or somebody

> Ms. Cadbury has been with this firm for 35 years. She is esteemed by everybody who has ever worked with her.

estimate to evaluate; to give an approximate cost or amount for something

> The carpenter estimates that the job of building those bookcases will cost us about $500.

estimate/ estimation what the cost or amount may be; an opinion

> We thought the carpenter's written estimate was a little high.

> My colleague's estimation of the competence of that new employee was higher than mine.

The Spanish word **estimar** is used for the two English verbs, *to esteem* and *to estimate.* Be careful of the difference in meaning in English.

fabricate to make up or create (typically a false story, a lie)

> I can't believe that everybody thought her story was true. She fabricated the whole thing!

In English, the Spanish word **fabricar** is *to manufacture.* English also uses *fabricate* for this meaning, but not commonly.

> That company manufactures farm machinery.

fabrication a lie

> What she told you was a total fabrication. And you believed her!

intimate   to imply in a subtle way

"Next Monday's my birthday, you know. Gee, it would be nice to have the day off, wouldn't it?" She intimated that she wouldn't be coming in to work the following Monday.

 NOTICE!

In English, the Spanish word **intimar** can mean *to become close.*

They became very close in college and have been best friends ever since.

invert   to turn inside out or upside down; reverse the position

The magician poured wine into a cup. When he inverted the cup, we thought the wine would spill out, but there was nothing in the cup! What a trick!

 NOTICE!

In English, the Spanish word **invertir** can be *to invest.*

They invested $5,000 in IBM. Now they hope the stock goes up.

manifest   to show plainly and clearly

The disease manifests itself by creating lesions on the skin.

In English, the Spanish word **manifestar** can be *to demonstrate,* and **manifestación** can be a *demonstration.*

The students demonstrated in support of a change in the university's admissions policies. The demonstration took place in front of the university gates.

manifestation   act of displaying, showing

The best manifestation of autumn is when the leaves turn colors.

molest   to attack sexually; to rape

He was sentenced to many years in prison for molesting his neighbor.

In English, the Spanish word **molestar** is *to annoy* or *bother.*

I'm sorry to bother you, but could you help me for a moment?

molestation   the act of molesting

He was convicted for the molestation of at least four women.

reclaim   1. to make land usable for growing crops or living on

The Dutch have reclaimed large areas of land that used to be underwater.

2. to take back

She reclaimed her self-esteem when she resigned from that dishonest company.

In English, the Spanish word **reclamar** is *to demand.*

Because the clock didn't work right, he demanded his money back from the store where he'd bought it.

reclamation   act of reclaiming, taking back

The reclamation of land from the sea is something that humans have done all over the world. This has increased the amount of land substantially.

regress   1. to go back, return, especially to a previous psychological condition

His mental illness made him regress to the time he was five years old.

2. to hypnotize a patient and bring him/her back to an earlier period

It was fascinating! During therapy, my psychologist regressed me to when I was a happy little boy.

In English, the Spanish word **regresar** is *to go back* or *return.*

After work, I go back home to have dinner and relax.

regression   the act of regressing, going back to a less developed state

The patient's hypnotic regression therapy is helping her find out why she has so many psychological problems as an adult.

renounce   to reject, give up

By the time he finished the rehabilitation program, he had renounced the use of illegal drugs forever.

In English, the Spanish word **renunciar** can be *to resign,* especially when talking about a job.

Because he had such a bad relationship with his boss, he finally resigned and accepted a job with another company. The boss gladly accepted his resignation.

renunciation   the act of renouncing

The rock musician's public renunciation of drugs inspired many teenagers to do the same thing.

replicate   to duplicate something through reconstruction or representation

Natural history museums love to replicate dinosaurs for their visitors to come and look at.

 NOTICE!

In English, the Spanish word **replicar** is *to argue against* something.

Many people in the United States have argued against using public tax money to fund private schools.

replica   a duplication or representation

The Maritime Museum has a wonderful replica of an 18th century Spanish galleon.

NOTICE!

In English, the Spanish word **réplica** is *rebuttal.*

The debate team leader's rebuttal to her opponent's argument was very convincing.

It's Under Construction

	return upside down
esteem manifest	intimate declassify
resign rebuttal	contest renounce
reclaim duplicate	fabricate regress
replicate estimate	challenge take back

Choose any two-word block. Write a sentence using both words. Write in pencil or erasable ink. Then choose another block and write another sentence. Keep going until you've used up all nine blocks.

1. _____

2. _____

3. _____

4. _____

5. _____

6. _____

7. _____

8. _____

9. _____

If you are in a class, exchange books with a partner. Read his/her sentences and let him/her read yours. If either of you finds any errors, discuss them and make any necessary corrections.

As I Was Saying . . .

Complete the following mini-conversations by using the list of vocabulary words for this unit. Each conversation has two speakers, Person A and Person B.

contest	*esteem*	*fabrications*	*investing*
declassify	*estimate*	*intimated*	*manifest*

1. A: The local environmentalist group is going to _____ the new housing project.

   B: I hear they're planning to lie down in front of the bulldozers!

2. A: How does the flu _____ itself differently from a cold?

   B: The symptoms are generally the same, except you usually have a fever with the flu.

3. My grandfather made a lot of money by _____ in Coca Cola when the company just started.

4. A: You know, the union leader has _____ that there might be a strike if management doesn't give the workers what they want.

   B: They should bring in an arbitrator before it's too late.

5. A: I hold our 6th grade teacher, Mr. Farb, in very high _____ . He is a very special person.

   B: That's true. You know, I _____ that he has helped over a thousand students to succeed in school.

6. A: I understand the Pentagon is going to _____ many records from the Korean War.

   B: I've heard most of those records weren't true anyway. They were just a lot of

   _____ invented by the government for propaganda purposes.

ALTA BOOK
CENTER
PUBLISHERS ID

14 Adrian Court
Burlingame
California, 94010
USA

Luis Quintero

Let's I.D. Them!

Work alone or with a partner. The exercise is on this and the next page. If you work with a partner, one of you has this page and the other one will work with the next page. Choose your page. Now get started.

Here's what to do if you work with a partner. If not, just write in your answers on both pages.

- Read No. 1 to your partner and write down his/her I.D. on the line provided.
- Then your partner will read No. 2 to you. You make the I.D. and he/she will write it down just as you did.
- Now you read No. 3 and keep working this way until you're all done. Wait for your teacher to review the correct answers and then score your partner's answers.

Each answer = 10 points.

Exercise A   **I.D.**

1. This is another way to say *challenge* or *dispute.*   _____

3. This is what somebody tells you if he lies to you.   _____

5. If an Olympic athlete is caught using drugs during the   _____
   Games, this is what will happen to him or her.

7. This means to make a copy of something.   _____

9. This is not top secret for the government anymore.   _____

11. This means making things in a factory.   _____

13. This is the value you put on somebody or something.   _____

15. Sometimes you go back to your childhood when you do this.   _____

17. You're doing this if you're calculating an approximate   _____
    amount or size.

19. Workers do this when they go on strike.   _____

Score: _____ **points**

Read the instructions on the previous page and you'll know what to do. Remember, when you score your partner's answers or your own, each one = 10 points.

Exercise B   **I.D.**

2. This means to create lies or other stories.   _____

4. When you take back something, you do this.   _____

6. This means to reject somebody or something.   _____

8. When you respect someone, you hold that person
   in high _____.   _____

10. When you let somebody know something in an indirect way.   _____

12. This is what you do when you give your boss a letter
    saying you are quitting your job.   _____

14. It's when something is turned inside out.   _____

16. It's another word for *rape.*   _____

18. This means to show or demonstrate clearly.   _____

20. When you buy stock in a company, you do this.   _____

Score: _____ **points**

Face to Face

Part A

Work alone or with a partner. Use this and the next page. If you work with somebody, decide who will look only at this page and who will look only at the next one.

By yourself: Read number 1 and then choose the best response from the next page. Continue through number 5, then start with number 6 on the next page and choose the response from this page.

With a partner: Read number 1 to your partner and he/she will select the best response from the other page. Continue until number 6. Now reverse how you do the exercise.

1. What's your estimate?

2. I hear she's in a mental hospital now. Is that right?

3. Are they contesting the judge's decision?

4. What's this I hear about replicating human beings?

5. Why didn't he get that job?

---

6. a) Yes. I'm going to renounce this job next week.

   b) Yes. I'm going to invert this job next week.

   c) Yes. I'm going to resign from this job next week.

7. a) No! He didn't molest anybody!

   b) No! He didn't annoy anybody!

   c) No! He didn't bother anybody!

8. a) Because they didn't want to tell the truth.

   b) Because they knew it was the truth.

   c) Because the factory didn't have enough.

9. a) By planting thousands of tulips.

   b) By digging a lot.

   c) By reclaiming land from the sea.

10. a) No. She only intimated that she was unhappy.

    b) No. She said she was unhappy.

    c) No. She's right.

Face to Face

Part B

1. a) Three hundred and fifty dollars.

   b) I like it very much.

   c) Bronze, I think.

2. a) Yes, she's having some plastic surgery.

   b) Yes, her therapist regressed her to the time she was an infant, but she hasn't come back.

   c) Yes, she's learning how to swim and use exercise machinery.

3. a) Of course. They like it very much.

   b) Of course. Their answer should be interesting.

   c) Of course. They think it's totally wrong.

4. a) It's called "cloning." Can you imagine having a new face?

   b) It's called "cloning." Can you imagine having such a vaccine?

   c) It's called "cloning." Can you imagine if there were two of you?

5. a) They declassified him.

   b) They disqualified him.

   c) They disappointed him.

---

6. Are you determined to find another job?

7. He's a rapist!

8. Why did they fabricate so much?

9. How did Holland expand its territory?

10. Did she tell you how she felt?

Index